NO MORE TANTRUMS

A Parent's Guide to Taming Your Toddler and Keeping Your Cool

DIANE MASON, GAYLE JENSEN,
AND CAROLYN RYZEWICZ

CONTEMPORARY BOOKS

A TRIBUNE COMPANY

Library of Congress Cataloging-in-Publication Data

Mason, Diane.
    No more tantrums : a parent's guide to taming your
toddler and keeping your cool / Diane Mason, Gayle
Jensen, and Carolyn Ryzewicz ; foreword by Vicki Lansky.
        p.   cm.
    Includes index.
    ISBN 0-8092-3070-4
        1. Toddlers.   2. Child rearing.   I. Jensen, Gayle.
II. Ryzewicz, Carolyn.   III. Title.
HQ774.5.M38   1997
649'.122—dc20   96-34768
                                                        CIP

Cover design by Todd Petersen
Cover photo copyright © ibid., inc./Marc Hauser
Interior design by Mary Lockwood

Published by Contemporary Books
An imprint of NTC/Contemporary Publishing Company
Two Prudential Plaza, Chicago, Illinois 60601-6790
Manufactured in the United States of America
International Standard Book Number: 0-8092-3070-4
10   9   8   7   6   5   4   3   2   1

To our families

Contents

Foreword by Vicki Lansky   vii

Introduction   1

1 Toddlers and Tantrums:
How to Keep Your Cool   7

2 When Baby Makes Four   15

3 Some Classic Older
Sibling Types   25

4 You Know I Can't Hear You When
I'm Screaming   33

5 The Taming of Some Shrews   45

6 Preschool Days, Preschool Days,
Endless Sets of Rules Days   49

7 War and . . . War 59

8 You Say "Dum-Dum" and She Says
   "Cuckoo Bird" 69

9 None for You, Three for Me 73

10 When Anger Becomes Mad 77

11 Nutrition Conniptions 83

12 Snacks: If You Can't Lick 'Em,
    Join 'Em 91

13 Truths and the Preschooler 97

14 What's That You're Hiding in
    Your Pocket? 107

15 The Kids Versus Ma Bell 113

16 "But Big Bird Is My
    Best Friend!" 123

17 Take Me Along 133

18 Bedtime Stories 153

    Index 165

Foreword

As I look back on the times parenting seemed the most difficult, it is not hard to point to the period—those early caretaking preschool years. The emotional and physical drain was tremendous. But how could I complain? After all, wasn't this the role I had chosen and felt was part of my destiny? And I was certainly not alone in this endeavor. Surely I knew I could do what everyone else was doing just as well, if not better.

Years later, I could finally put into perspective the different stages of parenthood I went through, along with the variety of jobs in my professional career. Then I finally gave myself permission to admit that taking care of my small children was the hardest job I had ever encountered!

I've written parenting books and a newspaper column, published a national newsletter, traveled, started a publishing company, been on TV and radio shows, and hired and fired along the way, but caretaking my children when they were small was the hardest job I've ever done.

It takes all the help we can get to survive those years. One of the best assets is a sense of humor. I think that is why I love what Diane Mason, Gayle Jensen, and Carolyn Ryzewicz have written in *No More Tantrums*. Being able to laugh at yourself, see the humor in it all, and still learn from each other is what makes this book stand out. It was written when these mothers were there—in the front lines you are experiencing now.

After a sense of humor comes empathy and compassion—the need to know we're not alone, we're not perfect. I believe there is some special mechanism in our psyche which allows knowing that to improve our attitude immeasurably.

Tantrums, sibling rivalry, whining, nagging, and fighting take a greater toll on the parents than on the children. They outgrow it and forget it; we struggle through it, trying to make something positive out of something negative. These and all the other common sand-in-the-shoe problems of daily life with little ones are addressed here. In addition to the humor and the compassion, you will find tips to try—can-dos to help you cope.

Being able to laugh and learn is the best combination. I know you will find this book as delightful and helpful as I have. You will feel less alone and more understanding as you begin tomorrow. I wish *No More Tantrums* had been there for me when I needed it.

—Vicki Lansky

Introduction

"I'm sorry, but I can't hire you for this job," said the interviewer.

"Why?" asked the applicant.

"Well, you have no academic background in this field, no apprenticeship, and no qualifications, and you've never done this type of work before."

"But I could learn."

"How can you expect to learn a job by trial and error?"

The applicant persisted. "But I want the position, and I'm sure I can do a good job if you'll only give me a chance."

The interviewer softened. "You're certainly sincere. Maybe . . . but remember, the hours are long, you'll make lots of mistakes, it will take years to learn, and you'll never be absolutely sure you're doing the right thing. Still want the job?"

"Yes. What will be my title?"

"Your title? Oh, yes. We'll call you a *parent.*"

Why does being a parent seem like an endless chain of happenings for which we're never quite prepared? Perhaps it's because from the very moment of birth the kids get the jump on us, and the rest of the time we spend trying to catch up.

True, we parents get lots of help. We get it from books, from doctors, from child development experts, from our own parents, and from the media. But very often the best support comes from our own allies—our parent peers— who are either standing where we stand or have stood there recently. We listen to hear someone say, "Yes, I understand how you feel. That happened to me." And we strain to hear someone say, "Have you tried this? It worked for me."

Most of us have a vague idea of our destination as parents and a reasonable definition of our hopes and expectations for our children. But it's that crazy winding route our aspirations have to take that hangs us up—and the thousand detours our children lead us through each and every day.

What parents seem to need most are ideas, because with ideas we get options. When problem situations arise with our children, it's so much nicer when we can react by choosing among alternatives A, B, and C, rather than always being stuck with not very effective A. And because we all seem to derive our best ideas from trial and error, we parents have within ourselves an abundance of data from which to construct positive, workable solutions to parent–child dilemmas.

It's time we pooled our knowledge, our experience, and our brainstorms. And if we do, there is sure to be something for everyone—if not a new idea, then the germ of one that will give us at least one more option.

This book is by parents, for parents, and about parents. It is not meant to explore in depth the causes of particular behavior in children; this we leave to the experts. Rather, it is designed as a sort of handbook—a helpful compilation of parent-tested, child-tested solutions to specific troublesome areas in child rearing during the preschool years (ages two to five). Our assumptions are the following.

We share these goals:

★ To control in our children the impulses toward negative behavior and

★ To encourage positive behavior, both in the sense that it is socially acceptable and because the solutions promote a healthy self-image.

In reaching these goals, we:

★ Often feel limited in the options available for dealing with situations;

★ Respect and seek advice from parent peers; and

★ Desire some concrete ideas rather than theories.

In selecting the preschool years, we did not inadvertently leap over the infancy period. The omission was intentional. This is not to say challenges are not inherent in the early months and years. In fact, some of the most profound ordeals of a parent occur during the first two years of being one. The care of a baby and the adjustment to having one can be dramatic.

But this book is about behavior and specific everyday situations that call for parental attention. In the first two years the child's behavior primarily tests our motor skills: that is, how fast can one catch a lamp that has just been pulled over; how quickly can a toddler be retrieved from the street; how does one divert a hand lunging toward the stove; how many spoonfuls of peaches can be shoveled in before she realizes they have peas in them?

Along about the second year the tests become more cerebral. With language and sophistication, children add variety to their acts, demanding that we parents call on every clever, creative cell in our bodies to handle the new barrage of surprises. Our theories, our goals, our grandiose philosophies about what we expect ten years from now—all are called into question by day-to-day happenings that defy any sense of predictability or order.

★ "But I don't believe in spanking," cries a parent as his hand goes out of control, seems to detach itself from his arm, and reaches out to whack the child.

★ "But I'm against giving kids between-meal snacks," protests Mom as she thrusts a cookie toward her squalling youngster.

★ "I'm flatly against bribing children," insists Dad as he plants a marshmallow under the bedcovers.

★ "Too much television is bad for kids," says a mother as she plops the child in front of the screen and hurries back to the kitchen to fix dinner.

It's the hour-by-hour drama of parenting that gets us snarled up. It's trying to translate our long-range goals into particular, concrete actions that bewilders us. It's trying to take last night's reflective rationalism and apply it to today's chaos. It's trying to hold to our beliefs and still get through the day.

We think the key rests with tools—their quality and quantity. The bigger the set of different size wrenches you have, the better your chances are of fixing the leaky pipe. The more ways you know to handle a situation, the better your chances are of handling it successfully.

Sometimes to get a complete set, we have to borrow from our neighbor. This book is written by all those neighbor parents—the ones who lend, the ones who borrow, and all the ones who share.

Toddlers and Tantrums:
How to Keep Your Cool

Temper tantrums come in all shapes and sizes, various decibel levels, and a myriad of duration spans. There are vertical temper tantrums, characterized by foot stomping and yelling; horizontal tantrums, in which the child beats or flails arms and legs in furious diffused motions; and total body tantrums, where the child begins screeching in a vertical stance, then dashes herself to the floor and beats hands and feet in a synchronized chaos of jerks and thuds.

Whatever method the child chooses, there are several truisms regarding tantrums. One: they happen to everyone. Two: they are a predictable part of a child's development, but unpredictable as to specific time or cause. Three: the underlying cause of the tantrum may be as minor as a mother's denial of a second ice cream cone or as major as deciding from which side of the car to exit. Four, and most vital: the length of tantrum endurance of the tantrummer (child) always far exceeds that of the tantrummee (parent).

It is to number four that we wish to address ourselves. Because there is nothing at all rational about a tantrum in terms of cause and effect, how can a parent deal with it in a way that allows some play for this very necessary emotional outlet of the child, yet leaves the parent's nerve endings intact? In short, is there anything a parent can do besides joining in the fray and throwing an adult version of the vertical tantrum (a last resort and quite unbecoming)?

We'll assume that most tantrums occur for the following reason. The child, usually beginning at about two years old, is beginning to learn the skills (and the difficulties) of decision making. And she is beginning to sense and assert a little spark inside that flickers with that wonderful feeling of *independence*. This, in itself, makes not getting one's way extremely unnerving to the child. But she's not verbal yet, rather, a physical being in everything she does. Thus we have the tantrum—an effective way to let emotions loose, vent all frustration, and shout "I'm *me!*" all at the same time.

"That's fine," we parents say. We understand. If understanding is the first plateau of tantrum solving, then the second is a veritable Mt. Everest. We still have to live through it.

Tactics for Tantrums

The following compilation of suggestions is based on the premise that some tantrum throwing will and should occur and that our job as parents is to make it as painless as possible for all participants. Remember, as one parent said, "If she doesn't go through this stage at two (or three, or four!), she'll probably go through it sometime later—maybe at eight—and then imagine the wear and tear on the kitchen floor!"

The Ignore Tactic

To use the ignore tactic the parent totally ignores the child's dramatic performance. Look busy. Bustle around the house, sweeping, dusting, or stacking magazines. Do not, however, try to read a book. It's best to remain a moving target. For the child, getting up and following the parent around takes a lot of steam out of the tantrum itself. The parent can try whistling or singing, something like "Victory at Sea" or "The Battle Hymn of the Republic" (avoid lullabies).

This method is listed first because it is usually the least effective. Its success depends on the parent's ability to outlast the child, and we all learn at some time or another (usually at 10:00 P.M.) who averages the most staying power.

The sequence of the remainder of the suggestions is arbitrary. Their success depends on the particular child, the particular parent, a bit of experimentation, and a lot of luck.

The "I Feel" Technique

Try describing the child's feelings to him. "Wow! You're really angry, aren't you? I can tell you're angry by the way you're acting (understatement). But I understand how you feel. Maybe you can tell me how you feel being so angry." Avoid asking why, because this is either unanswerable or opens a whole new can of worms; at any rate, it usually causes additional frustration for the child.

This technique can help encourage the child to express feelings and will hopefully begin to foster his ability to use verbal expression in the place of violent emotion. It also lets him know you understand.

Beware: this method requires calmness on the part of the parent. If you're not feeling patient enough to handle this, do not use it. Otherwise, you might end up like the mother who stood over her child screaming, "I understand how you feel! I understand! You're angry! Now shut up!"

The "I" Approach

This method is related to the previous "I feel" technique. For the child who is more verbal and beginning to reason, a simple explanation of the parent's feelings often helps; for example, "It makes me unhappy (or uneasy, nervous, angry, upset, bananas) to see you act like this."

This provides another context for encouraging expression of feelings in terms of "I." That is, there is more than a shade of difference between the comment "You are acting foolish and making me unhappy" (which labels the child's motives as bad or unhealthy) and a comment such as, "When *I* see this *I* feel unhappy" (which puts the label on the parent where it belongs).

The parent can also suggest that if the child ceases this behavior, she will make the parent feel better and happier. This demonstrates to the child that there are other feelings to consider and that she is capable of improving another's mood by a change in her own actions.

The Forced Exit

Forced exit involves removing the child from the scene. It works best if the parent forcefully but calmly takes the child to his room and announces that his behavior would be best suited to being alone. Thus, he should remain there until he feels he can settle down and join the rest of the family (or group).

This not only gets the child out of the social setting, but encourages him to realize that his kind of behavior is not being denied, only placed in a more acceptable setting, that is, in privacy. This has the extra benefit of helping the child to work through his emotions by himself. It also teaches him that he is indeed capable of exercising control over himself.

It is important to stress to the child that he will be very welcome to return when he feels better and that the parents or group are anxious to see him again. When he does rejoin the group, give him a warm, friendly welcome, and forgo the urge to get in the last word by tacking on a preachy phrase or two about the tantrum. In short, forget it!

Some children have been known to become so proficient at this method that they automatically go to their rooms when they feel a tantrum coming on, throw a zinger there, and return promptly, pleasant and ready for play.

The Goofy

Parents with a latent theatrical talent find this method quite successful. In it, the parent clowns, makes faces, dances around, sings ridiculous songs, falls down, or performs whatever slapstick antics come to mind. Not only is the child often distracted, but she may even laugh at seeing the ordinarily reserved adult acting human (or at least human in the sense that Bozo is human).

This technique is especially effective for the parent who reacts emotionally to tantrums, because it allows the parent to rechannel the urge to scream into more accept-able (however odd) behavior.

Bait and Switch

For the child with a good sense of humor (usually an older child of three or more), bait and switch is worth a try. The parent says something like, "I can see you're angry, so whatever you do, *don't* smile. Hold your mouth tight, don't let it smile. Oh no! I think I see a smile! Don't let your mouth smile!" It's amazing how often this con can be repeated successfully.

Diversionary Tactic

Try to divert the child's interest to something else. Pick up his favorite book and offer to read, or bring him a toy he likes. Children, especially young ones, have such short attention spans that they can often be distracted from their own performances.

If this doesn't work, try sitting down and actively play-ing with one of the child's toys yourself. Make comments like, "Gee, I'd forgotten how much fun this puzzle is. Look, I got this piece and this piece. Hmmmm . . . I won-der where this piece goes." There is nothing that quells a tantrum faster than a child thinking that someone else might be having more fun than he.

Retreat

Sometimes there is nothing else but to retreat. Let the child know you will absolutely not be drawn in. This approach is justified when the stimulus to the tantrum is so absurd that it is not worth any effort (such as the one that frequently occurs when someone fails to cut the sandwich in precisely the correct size pieces). No parent should be expected to waste much imaginative effort on such balderdash.

In this case the parent retreats to another room, bars the door, and waits it out.

Concession

Sometimes nothing works. And sometimes for reasons of sheer equality or common sense or both, the parent finds it necessary to concede. After all, we're not our children's adversaries; we're their advocates. Often, both interests are served by someone giving in. Giving in to a tantrum now and then will not foster a juvenile delinquent. Is the damage done by one extra cookie worth half an hour of wear and tear on both of you? Have you been unreasonable in the first place, demanding too much and thus contributing to the scene?

Sometimes a parent realizes soon after making a request or stating a vehement "No, you can't!" that the request is unreasonable or the desired compliance goes well beyond a fair expectation about the child. Now comes the dilemma. Should I stick to my guns, and make the point that when I say something, I mean it even if I now realize that what I have asked is dumb? Am I going to give in eventually, anyway? The key here is timing. If you know that sooner or later you are going to relent, then relent now. The more time that passes in the tantrum scene, the more reinforcement the child receives of the idea that persistence does pay off. The child may perceive that there are rewards to the one who can hold out the longest.

Most parents feel that if they give their instincts a chance, they can sense the times when it is best to give in, just as they can sense the times when they must maintain control. For example, the grocery store may not be the place to test our steadfastness to an ideal. Rather, it may be the place to graciously let our four-year-old win the cookie contest, especially when the alternative is to drag her out feet first. On the other hand, a tantrum thrown in an automobile, which could cause the driver to crash into a building, warrants parental supremacy. As long as a tantrum is not potentially dangerous, the parent may think, "It's been such a pleasant day so far. Do I want to blow it just to make a point?" As with every area of child behavior problems, it's a good idea to remember that our T-shirts may not match, but we're both on the same team.

When Baby Makes Four

"She's a real cute baby," said four-year-old Chuck a few minutes after his new sister came home from the hospital. "It's a shame we can't keep her."

When asked about the reactions of a preschooler to the arrival of a new sibling, parents are nearly unanimous on one point. There is one—a reaction, that is. Or, as a Mickey Mouse Club song said, "Anything can happen, and it usually does!"

In some families, little Chuck is not four years old but two. Instead of making a clever comment, he lashes out with slaps in an all-out frontal attack seemingly designed to permanently evict the baby. In another family, Chuck has a more inward reaction. Rather than striking, he sulks, sometimes going to his room where he systematically peels all the wallpaper off the wall. In other cases, he reverts from a completely toilet-trained toddler to a pants-wetting, bed-wetting bundle of frustration for the parents.

Most parents at one time or another try to see the problem from the child's point of view. This is most easily accomplished in the quiet of the late evening when the children are asleep (hopefully), rather than in the middle of a crisis while trying to intercept a Playskool puzzle that is whirling toward the baby's head.

One parent put it this way, "I think my child's feelings on the arrival of a new baby would parallel mine if my husband came home and said, 'Honey, I love you so much, and our marriage has worked out so well, that I want to do it again. Because I care so much for you, I'm taking a mistress. I know you're really going to like her.' "

And isn't this what we expect from our first child—that he share our enthusiasm, desire, and delight at the addition to our family?

Nonsense. Why should he be ecstatic? Who wants to see a period of total attention, an uninterrupted starring role, come to a screeching halt? No child worth his salt is going to surrender easily.

And on top of that, no matter how well we have prepared our child for the family addition, he will inevitably expect us to present him with a playmate—someone who can immediately jaunt out to the sandbox or hop on the tricycle and become an instant companion—another disappointment.

Most parents find that it is best to assume the going will be rough at first and then be pleasantly surprised if it's not. Our goal is not to deny that the baby will be a real blow to the child, but to find ways to make the blow easier to take and to set the stage for some rolling with the punches later on.

Mommy's Midnight Disappearance, the Baby-Sitter, and the Hospital Stay

★ The maturity of the preschooler dictates how much detail of the pregnancy and delivery should be discussed. Most parents have little trouble coming up with answers that work and are comfortable for them, especially since they have nine months to do it. It's best to stick to physiological realities. For example, tell the child that the baby is not in the stomach, but in the uterus or womb (or "special place" if you prefer something simpler); thus, the baby is not being smothered by the piles of vegetables and eggs you keep stuffing in.

★ Prepare the child for Mom's hasty exit in labor. Explain as much as the child can comprehend about where you are going, why, what will happen, and how long you expect to be gone. Certainly by now he is aware that you will be returning without the frontal bulge and with a new brother or sister.

Many hospitals and birthing centers offer sibling preparation classes as part of a total family-centered approach to birth. Depending on the facility where you will be giving birth, and your birth practitioner, your youngster may be permitted to be present during the birth—in any case, shortly after. A lot of parents find this is the optimal way to bring the new baby into the family.

Some women choose to give birth at home, accompanied by family members and in their own bed. If you do this, you won't have to be concerned about strategies for leaving or coming home, but make sure you get plenty of help with household chores, and perhaps someone to help care for your toddler so you can get rest.

★ Enlist the child's help getting the nursery and baby clothes ready. Let her arrange the drawers (if need be they can be straightened out later). Include the child in layette shopping, too, but make sure she also gets something for herself.

★ If your child will be staying home, choose a loving, caring baby-sitter. Daddies, grandparents, and close friends are tops on the list, and lucky are those who can procure their services. In any case, find someone with whom the child is comfortable and who knows the child's habits and needs. Or, at least, find someone capable of reading through the mountain of lists describing the minute points of the child's care (such as potty habits, favorite bedtime story, how you always cut pumpkin faces in the bologna, and how one must sing "Blup, blup, the milk's in the cup" before he will drink a drop).

★ Hold to the child's routine as much as possible while you are gone. Make arrangements for school, playgroup, or other regular activities to continue. Plan for the child to visit friends or to have playmates come over.

★ These days, birth is a speedy affair—a lot of parents are in and out of the hospital or birthing center in twelve to twenty-four hours. (Your toddler may not even know you've left home.) However, if your hospital stay is longer, communicate as much as possible with your child by phone or note. If the hospital allows them, sibling visits seem to provide a helpful experience for most families. Send home crackers, plastic spoons, extra cups, straws, cereal in individual boxes, and any other goodies from your meal tray that you can somehow manage not to eat.

★ When things have gone smoothly at home, most parents admit that Mom missed child much more than child missed Mom.

Baby Comes Home: The Power of First Impressions

★ Make some plans for homecoming. Consider having the baby-sitter or a friend take the child out of the house (to the park, for example). Then Mom and Dad can slip in with baby. Because most times are either mealtimes or naptimes for newborns, both can be gotten out of the way quickly and quietly. Parents who try this find advantages in having the baby fed and nestled all snug in his bed when Number One returns from his outing. The house is quiet, the baby has officially claimed his territory, he is sleeping soundly and thus posing no immediate threat, and there is now time to devote to the mother–child reunion.

However, if the older child is at home, have Daddy or Grandma carry the baby in, and make Mom's reunion with the oldest the focal point of excitement. There is plenty of time later to worship baby, examine toes, and point out familial resemblances. Also, clue in any doting grandparents who might be on the premises to temporarily resist excessive baby adoration. This is a time when slightly ignoring the baby pays off, and the baby will never know the difference.

One mother observed that her biggest mistake was to feed the baby immediately on arriving home. She was breast-feeding. The toddler was quite pleased with the baby, who seemed harmless enough, until his mother began to nurse. Seeing this, the toddler must have thought, "What nerve! This perfect stranger latching on to Mommy, all cuddly and close. That's just *too* close!" At this point the toddler took a healthy hunk of baby's hair (which for a newborn is the whole head) and jerked head and baby loose, causing much pain for both baby and breast and an unfortunate beginning for everyone.

★ When friends bearing tidings of joy come to call, they may not be privy to the devastation rendered when baby but not older child receives a gift. Have several small toys wrapped and hidden away; and if you spy a caller on your doorstep with only one package, quickly go to your stash for another.

★ Speaking of friends, we all know why they come. They come to see the baby, and they want to oooh and ahhh. And we love it. But make sure there are some ooohs and ahhhs directed toward the older one.

★ Parents bringing home their third or fourth child still confess to fussing over the infant as if he were the first. But whether baby is the fourth or the first, it is best to fuss in private or quietly. Long discussions about the number of wet diapers, ounces of formula consumed, or alertness of eyes and ears can be pursued out of earshot of the older sibling(s).

★ A baby doll presented to the oldest child (boys too, please) concurrent with Mom's homecoming is a technique most parents agree is tops. The doll does not have to be life-size, but it should be one that can be bathed and dressed while you are doing the same with the real baby. This is especially useful when the older child is still too young to participate in real baby care. The doll should also be durable enough to withstand being stomped or hurled against the wall. Remember anger is okay if expressed in an acceptable way.

★ There are many lovely children's books available on sibling rivalry. The good ones have sympathetic stories told from the child's point of view and often contain hints for parents as well. Other books tell about babies—what they are like and what they like to do. These books are quite helpful, particularly if read together before the baby's arrival. A children's librarian will be happy to assist you, often providing a list of books arranged by topic.

Everyday Brownie Points to Score with the Older Child

★ Stress the baby's feelings for the older child, but never the reverse, remembering that while the parents' love for the baby seems almost instantaneous, the sibling's love must grow and be nurtured. Four-year-olds see no advantages in blood ties, roots, or someone to trade clothes with in high school.

★ When the toddler comes into the room, you might say:

"Look! Baby Jon got excited when he saw you!" (This is easily accepted, because newborns wiggle a lot and always look excited.)

"He's smiling, I think. It must be because he heard your voice."

"Ann, the baby's watching you. He can hardly wait until you can teach him that game."

Involve the child in a way that emphasizes his importance. "I think Baby Jon needs a toy to look at. Could you pick one out? He always likes the ones you choose best."

Note: Toddlers tend to smush objects directly into babies' faces when showing them. Explain that it is much easier for baby to see all the pretty colors when the toy is held a little further out. Also, toddlers have been known to bury babies in a heap of toy offerings. Suggest that he select one toy at a time so the baby can see each one better, and make the toy presentation one of the big events of the day.

★ Be an opportunist. If baby ever stops crying at any time that can be coincided with the older child's presence, jump on the chance to suggest that he must have been comforted by the older one's arrival on the scene.

★ Avoid forcing the older child to kiss, hug, or show any loving emotions toward the baby. These scenes make cute pictures, but are an invasion of the child's private emotional realm and her right to love in her own way and in her own sweet time. If the overtures come spontaneously, however, act as warm and grateful as you feel, and grab the camera, quick!

★ Employ the older child's assistance getting diapers, bottles, powder, etc. There are many benefits to the child's self-esteem here, *if* the goal is to involve the child in baby care for the sake of the child. Don't make the child a "gofer."

★ Make the new family size a big deal.

"Look, there are four of us at the table. Count us. One, two, three, four."

"I've got two little friends in the back seat of the car. One, two. Two little friends."

"You're on my lap and Baby Jon is on Daddy's. Everyone has someone to cuddle."

"See my two little pals in the stroller. You look like two Twinkies in a package."

Some Classic Older Sibling Types

Classic Types

The Hitter

The hitter makes no bones about his feelings toward the tiny stranger who has usurped his position as hub of the family wheel. He immediately pulls out the big guns (his hands) and attacks head-on (or on the head).

The distraught parents must first realize and be comforted in the knowledge that this, too, will pass. Some parents, although quite distressed at seeing their precious firstborn abuse their equally precious secondborn, do admit that they would rather have resentment come out in the open than be internalized in a way that might more subtly affect the child's emotional development.

At any rate, parents of a hitter (or biter or kicker) must have the safety of the baby foremost in their minds.

★ Parents should try to discern when the trouble most often occurs. Is it at feeding time, when you come home from work, or when friends come to call? Then make every effort to keep the older one occupied or distracted during these times. Or, use these times to give her an extra dose of TLC (tender loving care).

★ Give a hitter few opportunities. Under no circumstances leave the baby alone with the child, although this protection must be subtle. It is best if the child does not suspect that the parents don't trust him yet.

★ As the situation improves, leave baby and child alone for short trial periods, with secret parental supervision from around the corner.

★ Stress baby's love for the child. "I can tell Jon loves you by his smile when he sees you." By emphasizing the baby's love, the child may begin to feel wanted and needed by the infant.

★ Talk about hands and the unacceptable versus acceptable things hands can do. For example, hands can play, eat, help Mommy with baby, pat baby, clap; but hands should not hit or shove. Take the child's hands and show him how to gently stroke the baby, saying, "Oh look, she really likes that!" Or, play the touch game: "Mommy touches you. See how gentle? Now you touch me. Good. That was gentle"; or, "That's a little hard. Be gentle. Now I touch you."

★ If the child seems determined to blast someone, encourage him to take his anger out on a pillow, the couch, or a toy punching bag. This shows that venting anger is okay but must be kept within acceptable limits. Explain that pillows don't get hurt and cry like real people do. Make sure the child is getting plenty of vigorous exercise (outside, if possible) to use up excess "mad" energy.

★ Decide how much hostility can be tolerated before you feel warranted in taking more aggressive action. For example, if you can handle a few pushes or swipes with a verbal reprimand, fine. If you've decided that hitting the baby over the head with a book goes well beyond a tolerable limit, then take the child firmly and calmly (if possible) to her room and indicate that she is to stay there for a while because her behavior toward the baby is totally unacceptable. As with many situations involving negative behavior, the isolation from the group technique is very effective.

Most parents find that if they make their limits clear and hold to them consistently, much of the negative behavior dwindles.

The Toilet-Trained Sudden Wetter

Many children, especially those recently trained, regress to toilet accidents in what seem to be deliberate attempts to create more laundry for the parents—exactly what they don't need!

Some parents feel that the best thing to do is to put the older child back into diapers, observing, "Big boys stay dry, babies don't, so they need diapers." But this method can be tricky. Unless handled correctly, it often can wreak havoc with a child's self-concept. Treat the move non-judgmentally, with great understanding, and not as a punishment of any kind. The parent should act as if it doesn't matter at all which the child chooses; but, if he does indeed choose to wet, he should probably be in diapers.

If we understand that what the child really wants is to be like the baby, there may be a less extreme method and one that does not create double diaper duty for the parent. Look at the situation through the child's eyes. When the parents change the baby, they smile, coo, stroke, and fuss. That's what the older one wants. So try changing his clothes on the baby's changing table or mat, and smile, giggle, and fuss over him as you do with the baby. Throw in a few sprinkles of baby powder for good measure. Sometimes this is all it takes!

The Sulker, the Seether, and the Opportunist Misbehaver

These types are grouped together because they all have one thing in common. The obvious jealousy and resentment of the baby do not come out in overt, aggressive behavior toward parents or baby; rather, the feelings seem to be held inside, producing mopiness or mischief. Although this will pass in time, it is nevertheless unnerving to parents who expect at any moment a total eruption from this live, steaming volcano.

Unless the child is very young, an attempt at verbal expression often helps. "You seem sad today. Can you tell me why? Is it because I have to spend so much time with the baby? I think I understand how you feel. It's rough when you want somebody's attention and they're doing something else." This talk should be followed up with specific times reserved for parent and older child only.

Some children seem very well adjusted on the surface but are often caught rendering a completely out-of-character destruction of house or property.

One mother, occupied with the new baby, suddenly realized that her eldest had been very quiet for some time. She sought her out, found her in her room, and was delighted with her efforts toward independent play. As she left the room, she thought, "Something is different in there." It was ten minutes later when she realized that the carpet was gone! The child had systematically removed the carpet squares and stacked them in the closet.

Perhaps topping this tale is the one about the enterprising toddler who one by one flushed the baby's diapers down the toilet until the entire sewer system was clogged. If one removes the diapers, he must have reasoned, then the baby will have to leave too. ("Ain't misbehavin', just wantin' more love from you.")

The "Me Want Bottle, Too" Child

Similar to the technique for the sudden wetter, the "Me want bottle, too" child can be humored and given a bottle. But remember to give all liquids, even at mealtimes, in a bottle. She will soon tire of this very slow, laborious process of obtaining refreshment. She will then often drop the request, feeling sorry for the baby, who has not yet learned the efficiency of drinking from a cup.

The Misdirected Playmate Pusher

The playmate pusher, somewhat like the misbehaver, appears well-adjusted and loving in the baby's presence at home. But send him out to play or to nursery school, and watch out! All the pent-up hostility toward the baby is lowered on unsuspecting playmates, who find themselves ducking blows not meant for them at all.

In this case, the parents may have been too pushy at home, expecting the child's instant acceptance of the baby and giving the child cues that tell him to button-up at home. Parents who prefer to have their child's aggression erupt at home rather than in public might consider opening up some more communication channels, showing the child that his negative feelings will be understood.

The Parent Hitter

In this scenario, the anger is directed at one or both parents. Most parents willingly take the blows if the alternative is that the baby will get them, figuring that as adults they have more resilience (this may or may not be the case).

The techniques used for the hitter apply here, with emphasis on understanding and outward acceptance of the child's negative feelings. "Are you angry with me because I gave the baby so much attention today? When you were a baby, I did the same things for you. Babies are such silly things; they need so much and they cry so much. It gets frustrating, doesn't it? But she'll grow up, just like you did, and things will get better soon. And anyway, tomorrow you and I are going to the park—just the two of us!"

The One-Way Streeter

Some children single out one person (usually a parent or grandparent) and reject all others. They then latch on to that one person with extreme jealous possessiveness. Frequently the chosen person is Daddy, from whom the child demands undivided attention, often going into a fit when Daddy so much as glances at the baby. It is as if the child is saying, "I want *one* person who still completely belongs to me. Mommy is a lost cause; she's in Babyville. But there's still a chance with Daddy."

One parent observed that during a conversation about family size the child was willing to surrender Mommy and Daddy both, but clung adamantly to Grandma. "You're my Mommy and Jon's Mommy. You're my Daddy and Jon's Daddy. But she's *my* Grandma!"

Most parents don't solve this. They wait it out. In the meantime, it helps if the chosen person both limits his or her intimacies with the baby until the eldest is in bed or out of earshot and instead lavishes extra attention on the eldest. Why add fuel to a fire that will fizzle out eventually anyway?

Time Marches On

Many of the early sibling problems diminish as the days and weeks pass. When asked how initial difficulties were handled, many parents simply replied, "We waited."

However, sibling rivalry never really vanishes. It just changes form. In fact, another surge of older child jealousy often comes when the baby begins to move around, do tricks, and in the process receives adoring applause from the adults.

Parents may want to resurrect some of the techniques used in the early days, only with variations to adjust for the child's increased sophistication. For example, by now the child can discern when the baby is and is not looking at him and when his presence did, in fact, cause the baby to stop crying. He also may be bored with the game of fetch (fetch diapers, bottle, etc.).

★ Make the child the teacher. Encourage her to show the baby how to do new things (eat with a spoon, drink from a cup, maneuver a toy, crawl, walk). Play on the child's gargantuan ego.

★ Talk about the benefits of being the older one. Enumerate the privileges the big brother has (playmates, going outside alone, bike, nursery school, ice cream cones). Let the child name as many things as he can that babies can't do and big boys can.

★ Let her help do major services for the baby (feeding, changing, washing).

★ Let him pick out presents for the baby or select the strained fruits and vegetables from the baby food shelves at the store.

★ Praise her for her kindness and consideration toward the baby. But don't overdo it. Children are quick to spot a con. Instead, let her overhear you telling friends how thoughtful and kind she is with the baby. Some children think the only reliable information is that gotten through eavesdropping.

★ Continue to stress the baby's love for the child. "Wow! Jon is so glad to see you! He really cried when you left for school. He sure does love you."

And what's more, he probably is, he probably did, and by now he certainly does!

You Know I Can't Hear You When I'm Screaming

In a home where two preschool children reside, a motto hangs on the refrigerator. It reads, "Save your big guns for the lions; use a flyswatter on the flies." Below that, in a different handwriting, is penciled, "Remember the one about catching more flies with honey than with vinegar."

For most of us, the word *discipline* connotes images of a naughty-looking child standing before a cross-looking parent whose arms are folded rigidly and whose foot is tapping in angry rhythm. Although scenes like this are played many times daily in most households where preschoolers live, the sentencing of unacceptable behavior is only a fraction of the discipline issue.

We like to think of discipline as guidance. This is no brilliant revelation; it comes from the true derivation of the word *discipline*, which from the parent's point of view might be defined as the ways we encourage appropriate behavior and discourage inappropriate behavior. Certainly this sometimes calls for punishment. Just as often, our disciplinary approach requires us to set examples, become teachers, and direct our children toward the ideals we hope for them: self-control, honesty, regard for others, responsibility, and respect for rules.

Theorizing about all of this is easy. It's easy right up to, but not beyond, the actual moment we spot the crayon marks on the new wallpaper. It may even be easy through the first forty-nine times we have been nagged at for a candy bar. But when number fifty comes, just watch those theories crumble. Day-to-day living with children demands spontaneous reactions to what parents often view as continuous harassment. Although our theories provide the foundation, they must also be translated into concrete trump cards that are effective and can be pulled quickly. And, as with guns, flyswatters, and honey, our methods must be appropriate. They must fit the deed and the child's level of understanding and development. They must be handled in a way that has few punitive overtones and more instructive ones. It is what the parent has up his or her sleeve that makes the difference between the teacher and the screecher.

Discipline Basics

Where a 50¢ Word Beats a 5¢ One

The terms *unacceptable* and *acceptable* seem like terribly big words for a two-year-old's vocabulary. Why not stick to the good ol' monosyllabic standbys *good* and *bad*? That's a good (acceptable) question.

Most misdeeds committed by preschoolers are just that: misdeeds. They are errors in judgment, independence-asserting defiance, rebellion against rules, and the learning process. Labeling these acts as bad seems to cut pretty deep. It suggests that there is an underlying motive that is deliberately corrupt. And it very quickly leads to the devastating labels of "bad girl" and "bad boy."

If parents can introduce the terms *unacceptable* and *acceptable* into vocabularies early, these words can become automatic to both parents and children. And these words do a lot better job of getting to the heart of the matter. "Your behavior is totally unacceptable" says to the child that "your *actions* are inappropriate to the situation; *I* do not accept them; but you are *not*, however, a bad person." When parents overhear their youngster calling another "bad boy" or "bad girl," they might hammer the point a bit further home by interjecting, "No. Susie is not a bad person. Perhaps she did an unacceptable thing. But she is not bad. No one is bad. It's only the things we do that sometimes are not acceptable." Why not save "bad" as a big gun for poisons, mean dogs, and the guys who ride the black horses?

Yakety-Yak, Don't Talk Back

Whoever would have thought that preschoolers could take a simple two-letter word and come up with such a variety of deliveries? Most common is the emphatic "NO!" Then comes the matter-of-fact *no* indicating the issue is closed. There is the head-shaking, usually drawn out *"noo-o-o-o-o."* There is the *"No, not me"* indicating that no matter what everyone else is doing, there will be no cooperation here. There is the blanket *no*, which means that anything requested in a twenty-four-hour period will be denied. And there is the vehement *no*, which is accompanied by flailing arms and kicking feet. One polite preschooler even says *"no, thank you."* This can go on ad infinitum, until the parent finally becomes totally paranoid and decides that "Yes, the child is out to get me."

The word *no* does not travel on a one-way street. Often our problems come when we say no. The parent says, "No, no more cookies," to which the two-year-old responds with yelping and the three-year-old with two-hundred-and-fifty choruses of, "Why?" Other times, it seems as if the child has gotten out of bed with both fists extended for a fight—any fight, just let me have a fight. The parent feels like a gentle Airedale being nipped at by a feisty Chihuahua. How long can the big dog shake the little one off his leg and walk calmly on?

When parents wail, "It's been a terrible day; I'm going crazy," they most often are talking about a day of defiance, belligerence, and general disagreeableness. We all have bad days, days when we feel out of sorts, but children seem to grab the lion's share of these. If we find ourselves the parents of a child who is especially hard to handle ("the resident grouch," as one mother puts it), we may need a particularly long list of ploys to get us through the day with a minimum number of crises.

Instead of pointing an accusing finger at either parent or child, we need to give a little thought to what is below the surface. Although few difficulties are the exclusive property of either participant, some are more child created, others more parent created. Consider an example: A child wakes up growling. Everything from the kind of cereal to the placement of her spoon irritates her. The parent tries to be pleasant; she rearranges the spoon, changes the cereal, hums a snappy tune. Even the snappy tune makes the child howl. By 9:05 A.M. the number of scenes is climbing into double digits. The word *no* is popping up at ten-second intervals. The parent checks the barometer for negative atmospheric pressure and consults the astrology section to see if it's in the stars. The conclusion is clear: it's going to be one of those days, and it looks like a record breaker. So far we can safely say the problem is child created. However, if the parent decides this is the morning to demand quiet and solitude for herself so she can catch up on two hours of bookkeeping, then the scales of responsibility are going to tip. Now the parent is creating situations that only aggravate the child's ill humor.

Although most rough days cannot be accounted for quite this simply, it is helpful to take a brief look at the roots of the problem. Assuming that the parent is ultimately in control of the outcome of events, then understanding the nature of the events will aid in the choice of techniques employed to change the course of them.

Child-Created Situations

Withdrawal Tactic

When a child is determined to pick a fight and resolute in her will to bug you, a variation of the ignore tactic may work. It is best to warn the child in advance, because appearing suddenly deaf usually arouses more friction. "This is my final word on the matter. I am not going to fight. And if you keep it up, I am going to ignore you." This says, in effect, "I am not going to come down to your level of bad humor. You are not going to draw me into your feuds. I will not play cat to your dog." We need to remember that what the child really wants is attention. If we let her engage us in quarrel after quarrel, we may be fueling the fire. Negative attention is still attention.

The trouble with ignoring is that it takes a great deal of patience. It is a struggle of wills and can be very draining on both parent and child. The parent may become quite paranoid, thinking that the child is an adversary bent on driving him or her to delirium. We must remember that at this age, the child is doing little more than testing us, testing herself, and coming to grips with the sensations of her own disposition. If we think it's any more than that, we are assigning to our children motives that go light years beyond their level of maturity.

Expanded Withdrawal Tactic

Using the tactic of expanded withdrawal may put a light at the end of the long ignore tunnel. "I can see you are in a very disagreeable mood. I understand; we all have bad days. But I am in a good mood. It feels good and I'd like to share it with you. I would like you to go to your room, and when you feel that you would like me to share my good mood with you, you may come back. When you do, I'll have the crayons ready and we can color together." (Or, "I might feel like taking you to the park.")

Easing Up

Avoid asking a cranky child to perform little more than the absolute necessities of life. This is a day to make few demands. Make corrections and give directives only when essential. Forget the "pick up the toys" rule, let manners slide, serve favorite food for lunch. Keep opportunities for defiance at a minimum. Skirt confrontations. Put on an air of pleasantness that says, "I am impervious to skirmishes today. Today I am a pillar of delight. How hard it is going to be to pierce my armor of cheerfulness."

Putting Distance Between You

Sometimes no matter what we do we finally sense that we simply are not wearing well on each other. Maybe it's because we've been cooped up in the house for three subzero days. Maybe we're both bored with routine. Or maybe our chemistries just don't mesh. Nowhere is it written that we have to live in harmony with our children all the time.

Here a baby-sitter can come in handy—or an arrangement with a neighbor for trading child care, or inviting a playmate over. In any case, the turning point might be both of you seeing a different face for a while. If none of these possibilities is available, a walk outside or a trip to the park can put distance between you, and perhaps you will happen upon some new faces along the way.

What about the subzero days when baby-sitters are unavailable and friends are all hibernating? Then you may need to muster up extra energics and creativity to get the child involved in diversionary activities (crafts, building blocks, puzzles). This may call for playing with the child until she is absorbed in her games, then sneaking off to snatch a minute or two of solitude and quiet.

Parent-Created Situations

Mommy the White Tornado

How long can we expect our children to be tidy, undemanding, and obedient while we clean our houses? One hour, two hours, all day? We need to know our children's limits and be aware of what is a fair expectation on a given day. If we ask too much, we are also asking for trouble as well. This is true also for telephone time, reading time, or quiet time while we watch the evening news.

This is not to say we cannot and should not enlist our children's cooperation while we pursue our personal projects and interests; however, we must be aware that they have a limit of endurance, beyond which they will seek attention in whatever way they can.

Some days children seem to thrive on being alone, playing for hours while we read, write, or complete chores. Other days we sense that our activities are causing friction, so we avoid parent-created crises by postponing what we're doing. Most parents agree that the hardest days with children are those when the parents are under pressure to get work done and the children are obstinate in their demand for attention.

Fair Is Fair

Although we frequently can compromise our work schedules in consideration for the child, sometimes we cannot. There are tasks that must be done, or we feel that we are fair in insisting that we be given our share of uninterrupted time to pursue a personal interest. Then we can say, "I am working on an important report (or project, book, hobby), and I would like to finish. I need you to go into the other room and find something to play with until I am finished. The less you bother me, the faster I will finish. And when I'm done (here comes the pièce de résistance), I will read you a book (or go to the park or play a game)." When you finish, be sure to keep your part of the bargain and do it with flair. "Oh boy! I'm finished! Isn't that great? Now we can read that book!"

There Are Two Sides to a Parent's Bed, Too

Sometimes the parent wins hands down in the grouch contest. On these days, we often are the harbingers of hostility. We snap at the kids, we bicker about little things, we make excessive demands in not-so-nice tones of voice. Before long we find we have created monsters out of former cherubs.

It's important to acknowledge the problem to the child. "I'm having a bad day. I don't think I've been very nice to you. Maybe if I could have some time alone I could feel better. Then I could share *your* good mood with you." It is certainly not asking too much of a child to accept that others get in lousy moods, too. In fact, it may make for a more realistic assessment of the world, providing that the parents do not take the privilege of claiming a bad day seven days a week.

Stubborn Is as Stubborn Does

Often we invite clashes when we expect too much of our children. We refuse ten different requests in a row and expect them to acquiesce with adult graciousness. There may be times when the situation calls for compromise. True, all ten requests may have been outlandish—"Can we go to Florida today? Can I have a puppy? Can I paint on the wall?" On the other hand, maybe we can find one or two that are possibles—"Can I have an extra cookie? Can I have a goldfish?" Giving in now and then can not only smooth rough spots, it can often avert them. It also allows us to keep some of our big guns in reserve for the more important issues of the day.

When Enough Is Enough

There comes a time when the parent says, "I've done all I can. I've tried every trick. The child is determined to make me blow up." So we explode. Often parents wonder if this was not only what the child was hoping for but what she needed. Like a storm on a hot, humid summer day, a burst of parental anger often clears the air. There is nothing wrong with demonstrating to a child that continued haranguing will eventually bring on a very unpleasant scene. Parents are about as human as human can get.

As often as there are occasions for compromise, there are occasions for a parent to cling stubbornly to a point. For example, four-year-old Mike was cross and irritable. A very strong-willed child, he was exceptionally difficult to handle in this mood. Mom had been making every effort to be pleasant but was met at every turn by a negative response. After what seemed like a fair request—"It's almost time to get your clothes on for nursery school"— Mike yelled "NO!" and lashed at Mom with a piece of rope. "Hitting with rope is totally unacceptable," was Mom's response. "I want you to go to your room until you can behave in a more acceptable way." Mike went to his room, emptied his toy box and shelves, and hurled toys furiously against the wall. Mom thought perhaps she should leave him alone, but she decided that he must be prevented from doing irreparable damage. She also felt that his anger was so intense that it might frighten him if he were left alone to control it without any help. She was right. After calming him somewhat (with a firm, vise-like hug), Mom said, "Now we have a problem. You have made a big mess in your room. I understand how angry you were, but we must now think about cleaning up the mess before you go to school." When this brought more angry protests from Mike, Mom said, "Okay, then, I will help you. We'll do it together."

"NO!"

"I'm afraid I can't fix lunch or let you go to school

until this mess is straightened up. It's all right to be angry sometimes, but when it's over we must be responsible for what our anger has made us do."

"No."

Mom got up and closed the door. "We are going to stay in this room until we have picked up the toys and you are dressed for school."

The response was not instantaneous. It was an hour-and-a-half later before Mike and Mom emerged smiling from the clean bedroom and hopped in the car to head for school. No effort was made to arrive on time. Although Mom never denied Mike his anger, she did have the patience and perseverance to insist he take the consequences of his inappropriate actions. In the atmosphere of love and security, he did. As for picking up the toys, Mom suggested a race. Of course Mike won handily.

Who's in Control, Anyway?

Living with children often seems like a power play. Although we like to be in control, we don't want to be despots. We want to be fair and concerned at all times with our child's rights, individuality, and personhood. However, when it comes down to the wire, someone must assume control of the family situation. By virtue of our position as parents, we not only are nominated, but we must serve. Our credentials are these:

★ We are smarter, and we're bigger. (Parents must be secure in their own authority.) We're also more experienced.

★ We are (hopefully) more mature.

★ Children feel more comfortable in an atmosphere of order.

★ Order demands leadership.

★ Children need limits. They want to learn, and they look to us for guidance.

Parents fare better when their leadership status is acknowledged. Children fare better when expectations of them are clear and firm. With both, we usually like each other better.

Some people believe that restrictions on behavior will stifle a child's growth and creativity. But isn't it possible that when the ground rules are fair and just, there is actually more freedom within this ordered structure? In other words, the more expedient we are in mastering the rudiments of daily living, the more hours we have for pleasure. The faster we learn the rules, the sooner we can start the game.

The Taming of
Some Shrews

Question: Who are often seen with clenched fists, bugged eyes, and hair on end?

Answer: The parents of a whiner.

Question: Who have been known to shout "no" fifty times in shrill succession?

Answer: The parents of a nagger.

On being asked when his child started talking, one parent replied, "Oh, he didn't talk until he was five. Before that, all he did was whine."

Whining and nagging are employed by kids for the purpose of getting something or somewhere. If it works, then it was worth the effort and will be tried again. With a few tools and a lot of persistence, parents can demonstrate that these habits will not work anymore. Persistence is stressed because whining and nagging are tough to eradicate.

How to Respond to a Whiner

★ Look for physical causes. Perhaps the child is tired or needs a pick-me-up snack.

★ If you feel the urge to give in, do it immediately. Then the child will not learn that the longevity of the nag attacks will eventually guarantee success.

★ Show that although whining will not work, a pleasant voice will. "That voice you're using really bothers my ears. Perhaps you could use your regular voice and say something like, 'May I have a cracker, please?' "

★ "When you talk in that unpleasant voice, it makes me not want to do anything for you. I'd like to get you that glass of juice, but why don't you try again in a different voice?"

★ When a child asks, unprompted, for something in a pleasant way, and if it is a request you can honor, respond fast and amiably. "I'd be happy to. How nice you were to ask in such a pleasant voice."

★ Make sure *your* requests are congenial. Often we reinforce whining by the examples we set.

★ Other responses to whining might include, "I'm sorry. When you talk like that it's hard for me to understand your words. Could you use your regular voice so I can understand what you want?" Or, use the knowing look approach, which says in a glance, "Would you like to do an instant replay on that? I listen better when I'm asked nicely."

How to Respond to a Nagger

★ Make sure you have been listening to the child. Children often nag because they have to. It's the only way to get the adult's attention. Answer on the first request whenever possible.

★ To the proverbial "How long before we get to Grandma's?" or "How soon before lunch?" you might respond, "We're not very close yet. I will tell you when we get pretty close so you can start to get ready."

"Look at the hands on the clock. When the big one is pointing to this number, it will be time to eat. If you want to go play, I'll call you right before the big hand is ready to be on that number."

"It will be a while longer yet. Because you have asked me this question so many times, I'm afraid I'll have to ignore you next time you ask."

★ To the persistent request for a denied toy or snack, respond, "I've explained to you why you cannot have it. I believe you understand. Next time you ask I will have to ignore you."

"My answer is final. I am not going to talk any more about it." Then by all means, don't talk about it anymore.

★ To persistence about a promise made, respond, "I told you we would go to the park when I finish my work. If you keep asking *when*, I may never finish my work."

"When you keep asking me over and over again, I get very annoyed. When I'm annoyed, it makes me feel like not doing anything for you. I want to take you to the park, but I want to go in a pleasant mood, not in an annoyed one."

★ To the ploy "Why can't I go to the park by myself? Susie can," you respond, "I don't know what the rule is in other families. Our rule says that you can't."

★ And to the finale "You are a bad Mommy (Daddy) because you said no," respond, "I'm sorry you feel that way. But whether or not I am a bad Mommy has nothing to do with ice cream cones. We do not eat ice cream cones before dinner."

Preschool Days,
Preschool Days,
Endless Sets of Rules Days

From discouraging crayoned murals on the bedroom wall to eliminating smushed gum in the living room, parents of preschoolers are constantly demanding limits to behavior in and around the home. The difficulty with rules is that with too many rules the child's independence and creativity get trampled, but with too few the parents get trampled. One parent observed, "Of all that comes out of my mouth every day, ninety percent is in the form of directives: 'Do this. Don't do that.'"

First we must decide what behavior must be modified and which actions we can ignore by simply clamping our lips tight and letting it pass. Once we've selected the biggies, we can add a few new responses and some original one-liners to our repertoire to help us end the day sounding less like a broken record to our child's already deaf ears. What follows are a few scenes that hang parents up and some ideas for getting unhung.

Problems and Responses

Crayons

Problem:
A Picasso-like crayon creation appears on the wallpaper—
beautiful, yes, but ill-placed.

Responses:

★ "Crayons on walls are totally unacceptable!"

★ "Crayons are for paper, not for walls. Here is your
paper to be used on the kitchen table only."

★ "It makes me so angry to see these marks on the
wrong place!"

★ "I will need help washing this wall. While we're working, we'll talk about the *right* place to use crayons.
How many can you think of?"

If the child protests your response, you can answer:

★ "This wall will have to be washed before I can play
with you, before you can go outside, before you can
have any toys."

★ "When you write on walls I must wash your drawings
off. When you write on paper I can save them and
hang them up for a while."

★ "I can see you've forgotten the rules for crayons. The
crayons will have to be put away for a while."

Many parents find it helpful to restrict artwork to particular areas of the house (kitchen, playroom, at tables).
Then the child is less likely to find herself in the wrong
room with a bright red tempter in her hand.

Ransacking

Problem:
Your child has ransacked living room, den, desk drawer, bedroom bureau, or kitchen cabinet.

Responses:
Some parents give children total freedom for search and seizure of every nook and cranny of the house. Others, for reason of safety, sanity, or just plain order, prefer to preserve certain areas against the perils of play. This can be done by making boundaries clear in ways that are fair.

★ "This room is for adults and for sitting and talking. Your room is for toys and play. If you want to sit quietly, you are welcome in here." Most try this once or twice, then leave, pitying grown-ups, who never have any fun.

★ "Sorry. No toys in here. Toys are kept in the playroom. You're welcome to come and sit, but you'll have to leave your toys behind."

★ "These are Mommy and Daddy's special drawers. I will show you what is in there, but you are not to go through them. Everyone needs some special places. If you would like to pick a drawer in your room as *your* special place, I will not go into it unless you tell me I can." By all means keep that promise.

★ "Furniture is for sitting, not for jumping. Outside is for jumping." Many parents stash an old mattress under the child's bed to be pulled out for jumping play. Others provide a climber or mattress in a playroom. "That chair is not a climbing toy. Your climber is especially for climbing. Why don't you play on it?"

★ "Here are the kitchen cabinets you may explore. The rest are off limits." Many parents provide one drawer in the kitchen for toys and child-safe utensils. "These are my drawers. That is *your* special drawer."

★ "We eat only in the kitchen. When you finish your snack, you may come into the other rooms." Make sure guest children obey this and all other house rules.

★ Sometimes a child will protest, "But you and Daddy have drinks in the living room!" Respond with, "We are grown-ups. When you are a grown-up, you may have this privilege, too." Parents should be able to pull rank now and then. But don't preface it with a comment like, "Children spill things, adults don't." That's sure to bring Dad's glass and the child's self-concept tumbling down together.

Street Safety

Problem:

Most parents realize that children are not instantaneously trained for outdoor play. After two years of totally supervising our child's play, we can't one day leave her, walk inside, hop in the shower, and expect no deviation from the rules. Being able to confidently leave a child outside to play takes time and patience. The consequences of errors multiply when our child steps outside the door.

Responses:

★ Begin training early. While walking, talk about streets.
"Streets are for cars. Sidewalks and yards are for people."
"Streets are dangerous. Hold my hand to cross."

"Cars are so tall. It's hard for the driver to see shorter people."

"See how I look around to see if any cars are coming. Can you look real well and tell me when you think we should cross?" If you want the child to learn to trust his own instincts, then be prepared to wait ten minutes before getting the go-ahead.

"The light is red. That means stop. Tell me when it turns green. Then we can go."

★ Explain the child's boundaries and act them out. Games can help.

"The sidewalk is your line. You don't play beyond. Let's practice." Parent begins running and frolicking in the yard, then suddenly crosses the line. "Whoops! I have to come back. I crossed the line." He jumps back in acceptable territory and yells, "Yea for Daddy! Now *you* try."

Or, the parent runs right to the line and stops short, "Screech! I can't go over the line."

Or, he uses role-playing. "You be the Daddy and I'll be the little girl. Tell me to turn around when I cross the line." Expect to be reprimanded sternly by some theatrical three-year-olds.

★ Constantly repeat. Parents of a one-and-a-half-year-old can be recognized by their well-developed calves and their ability to run the quarter mile in forty-five seconds. By the time the child is two, the savvy parents turn to their larynxes and soon become expert at hurling their voices rather than their bodies from the porch to the street. These comments work best if they are brief and of a positive nature, and are followed by a "Thank you" when the child complies.

"Turn around."

"That's far enough."

"This side of the line, please."

"Stop."

One parent refers to herself as the neighborhood echo, and has suggested that a recording of her voice bellowing "turn around" at five minute intervals could be placed in a window to supervise a whole afternoon of outdoor play.

Not to suggest a relationship between the child and Pavlov's puppy, but a parent can consider the efforts successful if, when the child reaches the boundary line, she mutters "far enough" to herself, turns around, and flashes a puzzled look toward the silent house.

★ Deal firmly with wanderers. Straying cannot be tolerated. This is a life or death matter and no time to be a nice guy. Deprivation by way of an afternoon spent in the house (no exceptions) is an apt punishment. "I can see you've forgotten the rules for outdoor play. I guess you'll have to spend the rest of the day inside until you can learn to remember the rules."

Apron Strings

Problem:

The time has come to lengthen the apron strings for the older child. She is trustworthy near the street, she is able to understand rules and boundaries, and she wants to visit her best friend in the next block. Depending on the neighborhood, it may be possible for her to walk there on her own.

Responses:

Expansion of boundaries on a gradual basis seems to work best. New territory doled out morsel by morsel will seem extra special, and the proud child is likely to respond with a burst of ability to handle the new responsibility these freedoms demand.

★ Describe new privileges with stress on the positive. "Look how far you can go now that you're three (or four or five). You may now go to Mary's house alone, and you may cross the street to Jeff's house if I am watching."

  "I'm sorry, but you can't cross Oak Street. But you *can* cross Maple and Elm. That's two streets you can cross because you're four!"

★ Call ahead for reservations. When a child is heading for a neighbor's house, call the parent and announce him. Ask the parent to call you if the child does not arrive within a reasonable period of time. Also, ask the parent to call you when the child leaves for home. Although the child does not have to know you are tracking him, one check is worth a thousand ulcers. When the child's capabilities are firmly established, this procedure can be dropped.

★ Make rules brief and clear. One preschooler, ready to embark on her maiden journey to a friend's house, was told by her mother, "Go straight to Brian's house. If he can't play, come straight home. Be sure to stay on the sidewalk. You don't have to cross any streets to go to his house, so don't cross any streets. Do you remember which house it is? It's the red one. When you are ready to come home, tell Mrs. Miller you are leaving and come straight home. Don't talk to any strangers. And, have fun!"

The child hesitated. "What's wrong?" asked the mother.

"I've changed my mind. I think I'll stay home." She might have added, "Where life is far simpler."

Most children perform best with only a few rules to master at a time. Use illustrations because she can't read yet. Post the rules on the door, the refrigerator, or another frequented spot. Design the rules

together with the child, let her draw or color them, and have her learn them by number.

This method also adds variety to a reprimand.

★ "What rule are you forgetting? Let's go check our list and see."

★ "I see you've forgotten Rule 2. Perhaps you should stay inside for a while until you can follow all of our outdoor rules."

★ "Rule 3 specifically says that . . ."

War and . . . War

VIOLENCE PLAGUES SANDBOX

Hostilities erupted late today in the small blue and yellow sandbox at the north corner of the E. H. Sandler backyard. Several witnesses observed Alyce Sandler, 3, and Cathy Washinsky, 4, bop each other on the head with shovels in an attempt to determine who had the bucket first.

"She stole my bucket," accused Sandler. "I was using it first!"

Washinsky retorted, "It's *my* bucket! I brought it from home."

Although the sandbox itself was unavailable for comment, two members of the United Neighborhood Peace-keeping Force consented to an interview.

Eric Sandler, father of Alyce and part-owner of the sandbox, said, "I didn't actually see what happened, but these fights go on all the time lately. The girls don't seem to be able to play together for more than two minutes without a flare-up."

Carol Washinsky, Cathy's mother, said, "The red bucket does belong to us, but I really can't say who was using it at the time in question."

Following a cease-fire, the opposing camps have bivouacked for the night. Peace talks are scheduled for the morning.

Try as we might to convince children that peace is far preferable to war and that the Golden Rule applies to *everyone*, we can spend an inordinate amount of time refereeing skirmishes. On some days it would be entirely fitting for us to don black and white shirts and charge around with whistles hanging from our necks.

Fighting can drive even the calmest of us crazy. Yet this behavior is as much a part of a child's repertoire as is relating harmoniously with his peers. Even though we accept fighting as a natural part of a child's immaturity, we cannot ignore it. Does this mean that parents are consigned to twenty-odd years on the border patrol? Not at all, according to the many veterans of childhood wars.

The key is selective intervention. Teach what is acceptable and unacceptable behavior. Match expectations to the child's age and maturity. Become involved when an injury (the child's) or a nervous breakdown (yours) appears imminent. Otherwise remove yourself from the scene, secure in the knowledge that this is not *your* problem.

Capital Offenses

Scratching, hitting, biting, kicking, or pummeling with a shovel—and any other novel form of physical violence—cannot be tolerated, whether our child is the aggressor or the one serving as the punching bag.

Spanking a child for hitting is at best a vent for our own anger and at worst hypocritical and confusing to the offender. It's all right if I (the parent) hit. But if you (the child) do, it's a punishable offense. This may be the lesson taught. This lesson suggests that standards of right and wrong vary according to a person's size and power.

Try getting out of that one twelve years hence when your son, the 6-foot 4-inch, 220-pound lineman, decides that he doesn't agree with an edict you've just handed down!

What then, are our alternatives if we decide to put our physical dominance on hold in the interest of setting a good example? First, try to determine the cause of the fight.

★ Is it the time of day for an attack of the grumpies? Is this just a bad day altogether? Are the children getting tired of this kind of play, tired of each other, or simply tired?

★ Do we have here yet another flare-up of sibling rivalry hostilities?

★ Are there age differences that might be frustrating, particularly to the youngest?

★ Does Blake just not get along with the little girl down the block?

In situations such as these, a reasonable response might be simply to take the child out of the situation. Separate the combatants. Suggest a quiet time in which the child can be alone. Adults certainly experience periods when they have no desire to be convivial, gracious, and charming. See how far you get if, on a Sunday afternoon, you ask Dad to relinquish his soft easy chair and the final moments of a cliff-hanger football game for a rousing tour through "Candy Land." Sometimes expecting sociability coupled with amiability is expecting too much.

Accept feelings of anger and frustration, but teach other ways to vent these emotions. In the belief that certain emotions demand a physical release, some parents deem an inanimate object—preferably soft—as the house-hold scapegoat. When the impulse to violence strikes, that object may be pounded, pulverized, and told off until the angry feelings have subsided. This is allowed, children are told, because "This thing is not alive and can't feel pain."

Parents who hesitate to encourage physical retribution of any sort often teach their children to translate angry feelings into verbal rather than physical terms.

★ "Hitting hurts people. Use words. *Say* why you're angry. Tell him you don't like what he's doing."

★ "Shovels are for digging in the sand, not for hitting people. I'll have to put this away until you think you can use it properly. But I would like you to tell me about what made you feel so mad."

★ "I'm so angry I could tear a phone book in half. How angry are you?"

Some literary-minded parents value the technique of making up stories (homespun Aesop's fables) to illustrate points about acceptable and unacceptable behavior. The advantage of this method of teaching is that the actual perpetrator of misdeeds is temporarily serving as judge. Also, it's someone else who's in trouble.

"It's that little girl in the story who is misbehaving and hurting people, not me. Boy, her friends wouldn't play with her the next day. Didn't she get just what she deserved? I could have told her that kicking people was wrong."

But the story ends happily. When she apologizes and promises to kick only soccer balls and not shins, everyone wants to be her friend again. Maybe it's not Pulitzer Prize–winning material, but disguised in enough dramatic and gory detail the fable can be interesting as well as instructive.

No-Fault Arbitration

A disagreement that leads to an exchange of blows is often fostered by an inability to negotiate or compromise. We can't expect bargaining table techniques from a trio of two-year-olds who only recently identified the concept of *mine*. Battle-seasoned four-year-olds can be expected to know some of the finer points involved in deciding who gets to play with the bowling set first when two have simultaneously grabbed for it. However, even these veterans may experience a breakdown in negotiations if, for example, one of the parties would rather fight than switch. Here's what we could *hope* would happen in such a dispute:

> *Robby (the host):* Hey, that's my bowling set. I wanna play with it.
> *Eric (the guest):* I wanna play with it. I got it first.
> *Robby:* No, you didn't.
> *Eric:* Yes I did!
> *Robby:* Did not.
> *Eric:* Did too. (Hands clenched, he braces himself to defend his rights.)
> *Robby:* (From vast experience, he recognizes the futility of this kind of interchange.) Hey, how about this? You bowl the first ball. Then we'll take turns.
> *Eric:* O.K.

More likely to occur is the following scene. We resume the dialogue after the first round of "Did not. Did too," and after it we mentally insert five more rounds of the same.

> *Robby:* Did not, not, NOT!
>
> *Eric:* Liar.
>
> *Robby:* (He is horror-struck at such defamation of character.) *You're* the liar! I'm *never* going to let you play with my bowling set.
>
> *Eric:* Oh yeah? I'm gonna throw it out the window. (He pulls the set out of Robby's hands.)
>
> *Robby:* Oh no you're not! (He performs a belly flop onto the set and Eric. The sounds of wrestling alert Robby's father to the possible seriousness of the dispute and he dashes in.)

Robby's father must decide among several options after pulling the two boys apart and reminding them of house rule 3—no fighting allowed.

He can try to get to the bottom of things, sort through the evidence, listen judiciously to the testimony, then award the bowling set to the most innocent (i.e., persuasive). He rejects this possibility as too time-consuming and subjective.

He can insist that Robby let Eric play with the bowling set first because Eric is the guest. This is tempting, but he rejects this option because Eric is as much to blame for the fight as Robby and therefore not to be rewarded.

He can punish Robby for fighting and send him to his room. But this again means that Eric gets the bowling set—this time by default.

He can send Eric home on the assumption that if the two can't get along, they will have to split up. Today, however, that option is out because he is taking care of Eric.

He decides to apply the technique of no-fault arbitration. He makes a short statement and performs one simple action. "Because you two don't seem to be able to work this problem out, I'll have to put the bowling set away. Let me know if you reach a compromise." He exits, carrying the contested article with him, leaving this impression: I cannot allow you to hurt each other, but after that, it is up to you either to reach an agreement or forfeit the toy.

The Art of Compromise

We can't expect children to apply techniques that they have not learned. They will find ways to resolve arguments only if we teach them specifically how negotiations and compromises work. First, they must learn the meanings of these words. Second, they must be shown various possibilities for compromise.

In the beginning, this does involve us as mediators in their disputes as we step in to point out some ways to resolve a problem successfully. After a few episodes, and once we see our children applying these techniques somewhat naturally, we can back off, intervening only when negotiations completely break down. At some point it would not be unreasonable for us to expect Robby and Eric to reach a compromise much like the one in the first version of their fight. At the very least, we can expect some attempts in this direction, however unsophisticated.

Here are some examples of phrases we might use to teach the process of compromise.

★ "You two seem to be having trouble deciding who uses the train first. Isn't there some way you can compromise? How about this? Mary sets up the tracks while Kristin gets the train cars together. Later on, you can switch."

★ "Hey, kids, since you both want to play with the doll, you'll have to find a way to share it. Hitting won't solve anything. How about if David plays with it today and Lynn plays with it tomorrow?"

★ "I don't like to hear screaming. Isn't there another way to decide how to divide up the grapes so that it's fair for everybody?"

★ "I see you found a way to compromise. Terrific! That means that I can bring out the other toys now that I know you can work out your differences."

Depending on age and maturity, children will learn principles of compromise at different speeds. On some days, they will forget everything they have learned and resort to the basic caveman routine: "I want that. (Bop.) It's mine." Nevertheless, if learning the art of compromise is consistently expected of them (and reinforced), children eventually will come to recognize its utility. It sure beats a bruised arm.

Bullies and Underdogs

Often within the family or neighborhood setting, playmates are mismatched in size and age. Parents can fall into the habit of serving as the younger or smaller child's protector. Of course, at times it is essential for parents to do just that. The principle of laissez-faire is one thing. Sitting back and watching your three-year-old get pulverized by Attila the Hun next door is quite another. The situation is one of degree. To constantly protect the younger or smaller one discourages the child from attempting to handle his own problems. It can also encourage the younger, smaller child to become manipulative.

Possibilities for handling the bully–underdog situation vary according to whether the confrontation exists within the family or outside it. If the bully is a family member, we can expect the child to develop more control over his tendencies toward physical aggression. If our expectations are not met, we can use whatever consequences are standard in the family: deprivation of a certain privilege, removal from the play scene, or whatever.

If the bully is the local neighborhood terror, possibilities for dealing with the situation are limited in some ways but expanded in others. Although you may not formally discipline a neighbor's child, you have every right to temporarily deny access to your yard to a child who cannot behave properly in it. Other options include the following:

★ Offer your child some phrases she might say to the bully. "When you're mean and hit me, I don't want to play with you anymore," or, "I don't like it when you do that."

★ Find children whose ages and maturity blend better with your child's. The underdog will often put up with the bully only because there's no one else around.

All these suggestions have assumed that the underdog has, throughout, shown sweet reasonableness and a peaceful nature that even Gandhi would applaud. This might be the case. However, the situation could be further complicated by the underdog rising. In this event, the victim of aggression takes the attitude, "I've had it. (Whap.) I'm mad, and I'm not going to take it anymore. (Oof.) Here's some of your own medicine, you bully."

There is not a parent among us who has seen this happen and not mentally approved, "At last Jane is standing up for her rights."

The problem, however, is that this type of behavior is what we have been trying to discourage in other situations. Thus thorny questions arise. When is physical retribution unacceptable? When is it necessary? How can we teach the difference?

Perhaps we do our children a favor by teaching them about situational ethics at an early age. If we feel that in some cases the bully–underdog problem would be rapidly solved by encouraging the underdog to defend himself, then we should also point out that most of the time there are better ways. We do not approve of physical violence, but we realize that occasionally it is the only way to deal with a playmate who knows only one avenue for getting his way. Until every child benefits from the teaching of humane values and until every child receives an adequate education concerning healthy ways of dealing with strong emotions, we seem to have no choice but to accept the possibility of last resort physical defense.

You Say "Dum-Dum" and She Says "Cuckoo Bird"

The Name-Caller

Children's penchant for name-calling is also an unacceptable manner of dealing with anger and frustration. All children do it. All children resent its being done to them. Parents must teach not only better ways to vent strong emotions, but also why name-calling doesn't solve anything.

We can explain that calling someone a dummy or a "stupid head" only serves to hurt their feelings, raise their ire, and leave them completely indisposed to amicable settlement. To encourage an appreciation for the feelings of others, we have to do a lot of talking about why "It makes people feel bad when you . . ." or how "It makes people feel good when you. . . ."

Good parental example helps also. If we parents are constantly referring to the next door neighbor as "old

69

motor mouth" or our mate as "you idiot," we are reinforcing these types of hurtful descriptions and increasing
the child's vocabulary of negative labels.

Teaching children more humane ways of dealing with
negative feelings about another person is a painstaking,
gradual process and one that will develop in a two steps
forward, one step backward fashion.

★ Remind children how hurt they are when someone
   calls them a nasty name.

★ Show an acceptable manner for venting "I hate you"
   feelings. Often, when children utter those famous
   three words, they're really saying "I'm so mad at
   you!" Teach them how to express that anger in more
   specific ways. "When someone does something that
   makes you really mad, tell her how you feel about it,
   such as 'I'm angry. You grabbed my shovel without
   asking for it.' "

★ Teach children their rights. There is no law that says
   they have to play with someone who consistently provokes them. If a friend doesn't respond, perhaps the
   relationship should cool for a while.

★ Teach children the beginnings of tolerance. No one is
   perfect. People do things that make us mad. When
   that happens, we have choices; we can overlook the
   problem, forgive the transgression, or make an issue
   of it and demand a change. There are many irritating
   qualities we have to learn to live with if we basically
   like a person. He's our friend and we would rather be
   with him than not, even if he isn't a willing sharer
   or loyal all the time or interested in performing daily
   installments of the "Adventures of Batman."

Teaching sophisticated concepts such as these requires infinite patience with relapses, as well as consistent reinforcement of successful applications. The following interchange between two verbal fighters demonstrates a relapse fostered by an unexpected response:

> *Jennifer:* Mommy, Katie called me a dum-dum. (The mother continues to read, refusing to step in as judge and jury.) Katie, if you call me a dum-dum, I'll call you one *forever*. Now, how would that feel to you?
> *Katie:* Fine.
> *Jennifer:* Then you're a dum-dum.

The Tattler

Reporting on the real or imagined misdeeds of others is yet another favorite pastime. It's a way of drawing attention to oneself or of focusing unwanted attention on someone else. Either way, it's intended to involve parents in childish disputes and to force us to act as referees (and just when we were about to retire our black and white shirts and our whistles).

There are two interrelated problems here. Are we being asked to solve a problem that should, by all rights, be handled by the individuals involved? If we take action, are we encouraging the growth and development of the family stool pigeon? Usually the answer to both questions is yes! In general, our tendency should be to discourage the tattler.

★ "Don't tell me. Tell Heather if you have a problem with what she's doing."

★ "I don't want to hear about that. I expect *you* to solve those kinds of problems."

★ "What Jeff does is not your concern unless it affects you. You be responsible for yourself, and let others be responsible for themselves."

However, there can be a slight plot twist here. What if the deed reported on is drastic enough that we must act rather than ignore the tattle? If we do intervene, how do we keep from positively reinforcing tattling? Again, situational ethics would apply.

Children are capable of understanding the difference between telling you when their own or someone else's safety is threatened (two-year-old brother is playing in the street) or when what they have to say is simply an up-to-the-minute report on the many injustices visited upon them by the world at large. Therefore, when we must respond to their confidential reports, we can thank them for letting us know because "Tommy could get hurt." On the other hand, when it is inappropriate to respond, we can cut their commentaries short with, "That doesn't concern us," or "I think you and Bucky can work that out." Gradually, they will learn from experience what we will listen to because it's important and what we will dismiss as not our concern.

None for You, Three for Me

Children are particularly inept at sharing, and understandably so. "Sharing isn't easy," said the forty-year-old as he polished off all the Halloween candy. To a child, sharing is a difficult virtue to embrace at a time when she can rarely see beyond the desires of the moment. Many a wise youngster has felt that sharing, which is so touted by adults, is basically your garden variety self-denial. Reasons the child, "Why should I share when by exercising a lot of smarts and a little bluster, I can have *all* the toys I want when I want them?"

No parent is without a story (or several) that depicts a nonsharer stockpiling all his toys in a corner and then guarding the hoard against visiting invaders with a ferocity Genghis Khan would envy. Most people don't really like to share, especially upon command. But we learn from experience that satisfaction postponed can often be satisfaction doubled. If we share what we have with others and they return the favor, then there is that much more for all of us to enjoy. Due to certain facts of life—the basic unpopularity of toy hoarders and the complete unwillingness of parents to sacrifice visits from all their friends with children—learning to share must proceed on schedule.

★ Reserve certain items as the child's special province that he need not be expected to share. With these special items adequately protected and free from prying hands, he may be more willing to relinquish (temporarily) what remains. Reasonable limits must prevail here. For example, we can't go along with the proposal that the swings, sandbox, and bikes are his special province and it is the grass that can be shared!

★ Make expectations appropriate to the age. To keep peace among very young playmates, it is often wise, where finances allow, to have two of some items. In the case of a playgroup, have paper bags with the same little things for everyone, or have piles of things to do where everyone's pile looks pretty much the same.

★ When possible, consult the child before offering something of hers to another person. This involves her in the decision and makes it seem less of a command from on high. "Would it be all right with you if Linda borrowed your crayons for a while?" Chances are she will say yes in all the generosity of power. But if she trumpets back a resounding "NO!", then we must be prepared to accept the decision because we did ask her permission. We can then say, "Linda would like to do some drawing. What can you think of for her to use? She's our guest and we want her to have a good time."

★ Consistently reinforce the habit of sharing. Ask one of the children to have an apple himself and to please take one to his brother. Before a friend comes over, ask the children to choose which of their toys (more than one, please) they would like to share today.

★ Whenever sharing has been spontaneously accomplished, identify it and compliment it. "You and Brad played so nicely with your friends today. I'm sure they appreciated your sharing so many of your toys and even some of Grandma's special fudge. I bet they will want to play with you again real soon!"

When Anger Becomes Mad

It seems that everyone has a friend who always stays calm in the face of all manner of pressure and harassment. If you happen to be this friend, you don't need this section because it offers some suggestions for coping with anger in acceptable ways.

The first suggestion is to forget the calm friend. You are you, endowed with a few inalienable rights—the right to life, liberty, and losing your temper. Given those rights, we must now decide where, when, and why we boil over; how we can keep our anger within limits; and how we can express it in ways which will be instructive rather than detrimental to the emotional development of our children.

A quota for adult temper tantrums would be meaningless. Sometimes we explode once a day for a week. Other times, we are able to sail a smooth sea for weeks. But given the correct combination of circumstances, most parents admit that their fuses will indeed blow. It is what we say and how we act when we're angry that create the very models our children will follow when dealing with their own fits.

A philosophy that proclaims "I am human! I can act however I feel, my children must accept my emotions" is fine for our individuality, but denies our responsibility as parents and teachers. In a family, there are adult roles and child roles. Like it or not, the child roles are filled. We are left with the burden of leadership. Sometimes this task cheats us out of the freedom to vent our feelings totally. However, if there are sacrifices in parenting—and there are—then this is one of the big ones. Thus, our inalienable right has conditions. We need to decide what kinds of examples we want to set and then find the ways to set them.

Before You Hurl Great-Grandma's Heirloom China Against the Wall

Avoid Stress

Avoid self-induced stress that makes edgy nerves edgier. The day your child is whining, nagging, and generally nipping at your heels may not be the day to repaint the kitchen, can tomatoes, or do your income tax return (unless it's April 14). Tempers tend to flare on days when we have a long list of projects and an extremely uncooperative youngster.

Bend Before You Break

Disagreements frequently lead to trouble. If you sense that an argument is leading nowhere except toward an explosion and the issue is not a vital one, give in. When our fuses are short it may not be the time to hold steadfast to a minor point.

Make Finality Final

You have just given the twenty-fifth reason why she cannot play outside in the rain. You glance down and notice your fists are clenched and your knuckles are turning white. You conclude that you are within seconds of losing your temper. If you elect to avoid blowing up and you are absolutely adamant against playing in the rain, then this is the time to employ the "No because I said NO" tactic, followed by an exit. As parents, we sometimes forget that we do not have to justify each and every decision. Not every *no* requires ten good reasons.

Say It with Words

We can show our children that there are many verbal ways to vent anger.

★ "When you tease your brother it makes me so angry I feel like boiling inside."

★ "I'm so angry I feel like kicking a tree over. That's how angry I am."

★ "I'm going to keep on being angry until you stop teasing your brother. In fact, I'm getting angrier and angrier all the time."

Some parents instill the phrase "get angry with words" into their children early.

★ "When Will grabs toys from you, use words, not hands, to show him how you feel."

★ "When you are so angry you feel like hitting, use words instead of hands."

When parents become so angry they have the urge to strike the child, they must get away from the child for a time. A child can be made to understand this and will eventually follow the example herself. Say, simply, "I need to be by myself for a while."

Pillow Talk

Sometimes our anger propels us beyond words into action. In these cases, remembering that little eyes are upon us, we need some ready outlets that show the child that anger is real and acceptable, but there are some acceptable ways to release it. We can:

★ Pummel pillows, couches, and chairs—soft things that don't cry or bash knuckles.

★ Stomp feet.

★ Slam a book down on the table.

★ Bang fists on the floor.

★ Punch a laundry bag.

★ Dash a ball to the ground (outside).

There are also some unacceptable ways.

★ Don't slam doors. You might have been careful that no fingers were in the doorway, but will your child be so cautious when it's her turn?

★ Don't throw things in the house. Even in anger you might be quick enough to distinguish between a Nerf ball and a lamp. Can your child?

★ Don't box walls. You child may imitate and make an unwise selection of a glass door.

★ Don't destroy objects. A four-year-old doesn't know what can and cannot be replaced.

No Guilt Trips, Please

Children need to experiment with their feelings. How else can they learn to channel them into acceptable outlets? Many children seem frightened by the uncontrollable extremes to which their anger carries them. They need to know that we accept their feelings and are willing to guide them through their angry outbursts with support and understanding.

By the same token, most of us would be left with little else to do but hang our heads if we felt ashamed every time we lost control. We are not superhuman. Our children will realize this sooner or later, so why not sooner?

An Apology Is Worth a Thousand Cover-Ups

★ "I lost my temper and threw a plate against the wall. Look at the mess I made. And it was very dangerous. I'm so sorry I chose the wrong way to show my anger. I apologize."

★ "I used my hands instead of words. I made a mistake in how I showed my anger. I'm sorry."

★ "I broke a house rule. I slammed the door. That was unacceptable. Maybe you could give me some ideas for better ways to show anger."

One Hug Is Worth a Thousand Strategies

When there is a conflict and a lot of anger in the air, one very good way to break the cycle and shift the energy is by simply sending love. Here's how. Remembering that you are the adult here, take a deep breath and think about how much you love your child. Hold an image in your mind of her being pleasant and lovable. Then reach out and give her a warm, gentle hug. Stroke her hair or her back. If she holds onto her anger and won't let you get close, just send love and imagine the hug. It works just as well. Later, she'll be ready to cuddle.

Nutrition Conniptions

This scene could occur in any home and at any dinner table populated by at least one preschooler. Embellish the narrative as necessary for the addition of other small participants.

The Boy Who Came (Briefly) to Dinner

Mike: (Age four, he seats himself in front of a color-coordinated dinner plate containing foods of green, red, white, and brownish hues.) What's this junk?

Mother: Why, Mike, that's your favorite hamburger cut up just the way you like it with ketchup on top. And you know that's mashed potato with butter. The green is a new vegetable we're trying tonight called zucchini. The red stuff is Grandma's Jell-O salad that you loved so much at her house last weekend.

Mike: Yuk! I hate this zuk stuff!

Mother: Zucchini. It tastes a little like a cucumber.

Mike: (Holding his stomach in preparation for certain gastric distress) I'm not going to eat this zucchini. I hate it.

Father: How do you know you hate it? You haven't tried it.

Mike: I can tell by the smell. (Taking one disdainful sniff and pushing the plate away)

Mother: Look, we're not going to argue about the vegetable. This is what we're having for dinner. (Employing the realities-of-life approach)

Father: Hey, son, your mother spent a lot of time fixing this nice dinner for us. Now let's show our appreciation and dig in. What do you say? (Combination approach: guilt trip and cheerleader)

Mike: That stupid zucchini is ruining everything on my plate!

Mother: Okay, never mind the zucchini. Try some of Grandma's Jell-O salad. You'll like that. (Diversionary tactic)

Mike: (Gingerly removing an infinitesimal amount of salad from the corner of the plate farthest away from the zucchini) This doesn't taste like Grandma's salad. It's slippery; hers was chewy.

Father: All right. Enough complaining. Just eat your dinner and be quiet! (In the authoritarian manner)

Mother: At least eat some of the meat and potatoes. (Compromise is not out of the question.)

Mike: How many bites do I have to eat for dessert?

Mother: We'll discuss dessert *after* you've eaten your dinner.

Mike: I'm not eating unless I get dessert.

Father: That's it! I've had it. Up to your room. There'll be no dinner and no dessert. You're not going to ruin this meal for the rest of us.

Mike: I wasn't hungry anyway. (Stated matter-of-factly, but he exits hastily)

If your Mike or Amy would have gobbled up most of the meat and potatoes, approved (with reservations) the secondhand version of Grandma's salad, sportingly attempted two small bites of zucchini, and finished up with several swigs of milk and a compliment to the chef, then read no further! By all means, don't tinker with success.

Most parents, however, identify at least somewhat with the characters who appeared in "The Boy Who Came (Briefly) to Dinner." What happened to the good old days of infancy when, with rare exceptions, all foods were gobbled up—even prunes and beets? How are parents to:

★ Build sound bodies twelve ways?

★ Campaign unceasingly for three balanced meals a day *and* nutritious snacks?

★ Wage the "war to end all wars" against sugar?

★ Instill proper eating habits?

★ Teach the concept of good nutrition?

By now we've all reached our individual conclusions about our children's nutritional needs (how many green vegetables and how often) and their food intake capacities (whether three large or many small meals a day work well for them and us).

We've come to know our own comfort levels with how much and what kinds of foods our children eat; how few ounces of fish they may ingest in a year without risking galloping malnutrition; or how few bites of food may actually find their way from plate to fork to mouth without our feeling intense, surrogate hunger pains.

We try our best to set good eating examples even though *we* certainly didn't have the advantages of an early nutritional education and thus have many bad habits to monitor.

And, we're all secure in the knowledge that a hungry child will eat. We can now move on to three pitfalls to be avoided.

Pitfalls to Avoid

Bargaining

Sad experience has taught many of us that, on a regular basis, we shouldn't make a big deal about desserts or use them as a bribe for finishing a meal. If we do, meals invariably become bargaining sessions. How many bites of pork chop plus how many chunks of apple minus how many tidbits of neglected cauliflower merit at least a small piece of pie? How about two chunks of apple for one graham cracker? Not only is the meal not enjoyed for its own sake, but negotiations rapidly reach mind-boggling complexity, especially if more than one child is in attendance. Keeping track of assorted numbers of bites might be useful for math practice, but it hampers mealtime conversation and relaxation.

The Clean Plate Club

Although our generation of parents theoretically frowns upon this remnant of bygone eras, in practice it is often hard to resist. If our children finish everything on their plates, then we can be sure that they have gotten a good solid meal, and we can feel confirmed as nourishers.

A secondary problem is purely our own. In spite of our development under the clean plate regime, many of us try valiantly to resist that inner compulsion to gobble every last morsel on our plates. Yet we feel somehow guilty about food waste. Is it not a transgression against the family budget, the economic condition of the farmer, and starving children everywhere?

Reconditioning is a very gradual process. However, there are encouraging signs. Many kids are now being recruited to membership in the I-ate-some-of-almost-everything-on-my-plate club. We hear rumors that parents are permitting their preschoolers to accede to full-up signals from the stomach. The best news is that children are handing their parents half-finished ice cream cones moaning, "I just can't eat any more. I'm full." Sometimes those half-finished cones even find their way to a garbage can!

The Authoritarian Approach

"Eat it because I say so." Many parents we know consider mealtimes the very last place they wish to test their mettle, their endurance, their mental acuity, or their powers of debate. Instead of nagging, threatening, or cajoling, they have found some better ways.

Some Better Ways

Introduce children to a variety of foods with little pressure but a lot of enthusiasm.

★ "We're trying something new tonight. Let's all give it one or two try-bites."

★ "Feeling a little doubtful? It looks funny? Remember that guy in *Green Eggs and Ham*? He kept saying he wouldn't try them, 'Nope, absolutely not.' Finally he did and he really liked them. Remember that? Boy, that guy would have missed out on something really good if he hadn't given them a try."

★ "You tried it and you don't like it. No problem. Let's just leave it on your plate for a little color. Maybe you'll like it when you get a little older."

To this, one three-year-old solemnly informed his parents that he would probably like vegetables when he was sixteen.

Try these variations.

★ Give kids choices of foods when possible. Note that this is *not* intended to put huge burdens on the kitchen crew.

★ Include in each meal at least one item everyone is sure to like, at least this week.

★ Try new foods or old standbys cooked differently. Even favorites get to be boring if they are served every Wednesday and Sunday.

★ Arrange foods in interesting, colorful ways. Cut out geometric shapes or adorn food with smiling faces. Be imaginative.

★ Use reverse psychology. "Please do not, under any circumstances, eat your carrots. You have four pieces of carrot there, and I hope that when I look again, I won't see only two!"

★ Involve the child in meal preparation. Often a few nutritional goodies get popped in the mouth and

sneak past taste buds not yet activated to full mealtime alert. ("Hey, wake up you guys! Was that a radish
that just slipped past our vitamin B rejecters?")

Mealtime Ground Rules

★ What is on your plate is this meal's specialty of the
house. Requests for substitutions or removal might be
viewed as an insult to the management (bad moods
prevailing). Ketchup may be provided upon request
(good moods prevailing).

★ How much you eat is a matter between you and your
stomach, which with any luck and the proper timing
of snacks will be reasonably empty. There are merely
two qualifications: one try-bite is expected, and, with
certain exceptions, the kitchen closes after dinner
and reopens at breakfast.

★ Eating small portions of a variety of foods makes for
strong, active, alert minds and bodies. This is a good
thing. Parents are pleased when good things happen
to their children.

★ There is a time and place for yuks, ughs, groans, and
"How could you think I would like that icky stuff?"
All such complaints may be registered with the chef
after the table has been cleared. Efforts will be made
for future customer satisfaction.

Snacks: If You Can't Lick 'Em, Join 'Em

We've never heard of a preschooler who could make it through a day on the go-power of three meals alone. It's a long, long way from noon to 6:00 P.M., or even from breakfast to lunch. This does not suggest that parents should view themselves as proprietors of fast-food establishments, dispensing tasty morsels at the drop of an "I'm starved." Many parents choose midmorning and midafternoon as the logical times for pick-me-ups—not too close to the next meal or too far from the last.

As long as snacking is a fact of life with preschoolers, why not use these golden opportunities to sneak in a few nutrients? There are certain snacks that parents rate as triple "A" because these snacks provide vitamins and energy but restrict calories and cavity-producing remnants: cheese, carrot sticks and other fresh vegetables, hard-boiled eggs, and peanut butter on anything. B-rated snacks do a good job in other respects, but are tougher on the teeth: fresh fruit, natural fruit juices (no sugar added), and raisins. C-rated offerings, although satisfying, have higher sugar, fat, or calorie content and lower nutritional levels: homemade custards and puddings, ice cream, and crackers made from whole grains. Sugarless soft drinks raise some thorny questions about chemical additives, and we should keep in mind the virtues of water. On the other hand, sugarless gum is a great pleaser of children and busy parents; we didn't say every snack had to be vitamin packed! Z-rated snacks equal junk foods, which are only for dire emergencies or to counter severe sugar withdrawal symptoms: all the gooey, sweet stuff (save allotments for trips to Grandma's), chips, most canned fruit juices, and sugary soft drinks.

> *Child:* I'm hungry. Where are the doughnuts?
> *Parent:* Sorry. I don't have anything like that today. What I can offer is cheese, a peach, or carrot sticks. Choose two even!
> *Child:* I'd rather have a doughnut!
> *Parent:* When I'm offering such a deal on cheese, peaches, and carrot sticks?
> *Child:* (Sensing that you can't get blood from a turnip) Oh, all right, I'll take a peach and two carrot sticks.

With a positive mental attitude on the parent's part and a fairly consistent method of operating, someday our children may say, "I'm hungry. Where are the carrot sticks?"

Peaceful Coexistence with a Sugary, Fat-Filled World

Herein lies our dilemma: sugar and fat taste good. We can pontificate endlessly on the virtues of celery stalks, yet, given a choice, ninety-nine point nine kids out of a hundred will probably prefer chocolate chip cookies. Given such an unhelpful fact of nature, how are we to promote good food when at every turn of the TV knob or the grocery cart our kids are confronted with the wonders of Twinkies, Kool-Aid, and Bubble Yum?

We can:

★ Identify the enemies: sugar and fat.

★ Maintain a limited household supply of sugary, fat-filled items.

★ Talk a lot about the obnoxious qualities of cavities and excess fat as opposed to the delights of healthy teeth and slim bodies.

★ Point out that eating too many sugary or fatty foods takes away our appetite for foods that keep us strong and healthy.

Teaching Nutritional Concepts

Many parents make a point of discussing nutrition with their preschoolers. They feel that it is important to teach the appropriate vocabulary—words like *vitamins*, *minerals*, *calories*, and *proteins*. By calling specific attention to good nutrition, they hope to build respect for its value. They are not timid about labeling junk food or praising grow food.

Curious children can thrive on the technicalities involved. One four-and-a-half-year-old we know asked her father about sugarless gum: was it junk food? "No, not exactly." Was it grow food? "No, not that either. It's kind of an in-between food. It doesn't particularly hurt you, but it doesn't help you either." The conclusion was interpreted by this preschooler: "If junk foods are 'no' foods and grow foods are 'yes' foods, then sugarless gum must be a 'maybe' food. I get it."

Another story we heard involved a five-year-old and a savvy Easter Bunny who filled the baskets with whole wheat crackers and cheese kisses. Scott was later heard to mutter, "Well, it *certainly* was a nutritious Easter!"

A surprisingly large number of parents say their biggest problem in properly nourishing their kids is getting too hyper about the whole thing and being overly conscientious to the point of making everyone nervous.

One mother explained in detail how she was able to lighten up and relax a little. "It finally occurred to me that I was getting absolutely distraught about the nutrition issue. I agonized over food additives, preservatives, cholesterol, and mercury content to the point where I was coming home from the store with meager supplies because I couldn't find enough things my family liked that were safe to buy. I was forced to come to grips with the fact that I had to live in a canned and packaged food world unless I was ready to grow my own. Now, I give the kids eggs, tuna fish, peanut butter, but just not too often. You do have to offer something other than carrot sticks or pasta for lunch!

"Also, I was becoming really rigid about what I considered proper daily food intake. The kids were getting balky at meals—I'm sure mostly because of my endless nagging to eat just the one more bite of whatever. An eating problem was being created—by me! So I loosened up on my expectations. I told myself that some days are just blown in terms of proper diet and tomorrow's another day. I'd look at the kids, see that they were active and healthy, and remind myself that they didn't need very much food at their age. As long as they weren't loading up on sweets, even one good meal could be sufficient. My relaxing was a relief to us all."

Although we applaud this approach, we should also admit that, despite certain statements to the contrary, we're all secretly hoping for the prompt discovery of a natural food that combines the nutritional wallop of a vegetable garden and the calories of a head of lettuce with the appearance and taste of Aunt Betty's chocolate chip cookies.

Truths and the Preschooler

At some point in their preschooler's development, parents begin to take a look at how the child's conscience is coming along. This usually happens when the child is three or four and the parents catch him in some clumsy attempts at concealing the truth.

★ "The doggie ate those cookies." (Aha! We don't have a dog.)

★ "My pants got wet when I fell in the puddle." (We haven't had rain in a week.)

★ "I didn't bite Scott, he fell down." (I suppose that's how he got teeth marks on his arm.)

★ "The leprechauns gave me these flowers." (Since when are leprechauns giving away prize begonias from Ms. Young's garden?)

Most parents, thankfully, avoid labeling these statements as lies. Preschoolers don't lie. They fib, they tell tall
tales, and they con us, but they don't lie. Their cover-ups
are not cause for senate investigations or parental insom-
nia. If we think they are, we are probably overreacting
and most definitely forgetting how immature a three-,
four-, or five-year-old is.

What is conscience, anyway? We know newborns don't
have one. If they did, they would never drag moms and
dads out of bed in the middle of the night. And a one-
year-old with a strong conscience would consider it
unthinkable to scare mother to death by climbing on top
of the refrigerator.

Conscience, then, must be something that is acquired
through growth, maturity, and guidance. It is an accu-
mulation of the positive responses one receives for doing
the right thing over and over again and of the negative
responses for doing the wrong thing.

Certainly a three-year-old's experiments with truth and
falsehood are not signs of moral decay. Rather, they are
the beginnings of the slow process of learning the standards and values that govern a peaceful coexistence with
family, friends, and society. If we remind ourselves that
the child is basically amoral at birth, we can keep her
behavior in its proper perspective and deal with it in a
way that is consistent with a preschool level of maturity.

Now comes the tricky part. How does a parent pry the
truth out of a child who is resolute in his version of reality? Children usually employ fibs to conceal unacceptable
behavior. How does a parent reward the truth yet discourage the behavior that prompted the fib? How does
one handle tall tales? A child's imagination is delightful
to watch. How can a parent give it room to flourish and

at the same time help the child distinguish between fantasy and reality?

Many of the answers to these questions are found in our reactions to fibs, our own choice of words, and our understanding of what led the child to choose fiction over fact.

The Truth Hurts

From the playroom comes the whacking sound of hand on body, followed by wailing from Tommy, age two. Mother hurries to investigate and finds Ann, age four, shuffling her feet guiltily. Because Tommy's twelve-word vocabulary is insufficient for a first-hand report, Mother turns toward Ann. With a "you're gonna get it" look in her eye, she says:

"Did you hit Tommy?"
Silence.
"Well, did you?"
A nod.
Mother turns red and yells, "Hitting is wrong! You will
    go to your room and stay there until supper."
Ann is dragged crying from the playroom.

Next day. The familiar whacking noise is again heard from the playroom, followed by Tommy's howl. Mother enters.

"Did you hit Tommy?"
"No."
"He's crying. You hit him, didn't you?"
"No."
"Then why is he crying?"

"He musta fell down."

Defeated, Mother shakes her head and exits.

From Ann's point of view, this is clearly a case of self-preservation. She has learned that a fib saves her from punishment. Mother, not wanting to accuse Ann of falsehood, has no other recourse but to let the matter slide. She has reinforced Ann's discovery that fibs are a protective device and has surrendered the grounds on which to deal with the unacceptable act.

It all started when Mother punished Ann the first time. In her immaturity, Ann concluded that the consequence of truth is unpleasant. Is this to say we should forego necessary corrective action in our quest to reward the truth? Are we taking the risk that the child will conclude that she can get away with anything she wants as long as she fesses up? The answer, it seems, is to handle the situation in a way that allows us to deal with both the fib *and* the behavior that prompted it.

First, the question "Did you?" invites a fib. It sets up the child, who must decide whether to tell the truth and face the music or to fib and go free. The parent, too, is faced with a dead-end situation. If the child answers no, the parent must either accept the answer or respond by saying, "I don't believe you."

A more open-ended and successful response is one that describes the scene as the parent sees it.

★ "I heard you hitting Tommy."

★ "Tommy has been hit, and you're the only one here."

★ "I believe you hit Tommy."

If the child denies the act, the next approach might be to talk around the issue for a while.

★ "Ann, do you understand the difference between truth and falsehood? You know how important truth is. Telling the truth is especially important to me. It makes me very unhappy when you don't tell the truth but very happy when you do. Now, is there anything you'd like to tell me?"

★ "Everyone does unacceptable things sometimes. The important thing is to be honest about them so we can learn to do better."

★ "Right now we have a problem. If you can tell me what really happened, I can help you. Then together we can solve the problem in a grown-up way."

★ "I promise I won't yell or get angry if you tell me the truth." (Here we must absolutely keep our word.)

At this point some children are still stubborn. In that case, you might respond, "I think you should go to your room and come back when you are ready to talk about this in a truthful way. Do you want me to help you, or do you want to go by yourself?"

One preschooler, caught after committing a misdemeanor and asked what happened would often reply, "I don't remember."

In that case you can respond, "I want you to go to your room and try to remember. When you remember, you may come back and tell me. Then you and Tommy can play some more."

Now comes the hard part. If punishment is called for, do we forego it because the child has been honest? It depends.

Most children are able to discern with our help that there are two issues involved. There is the issue of truth and the issue of behavior.

"Someone has used crayon on the wall."
"Tommy did," says Ann.
"Ann did," says Tommy.

The importance of truth is discussed, and the children are sent to their rooms to think it over. Finally Tommy returns to say, "I did it."

★ "Thank you for telling me the truth," the parent says in a friendly way. "I'm still unhappy about the crayon marks, but very proud of your honesty. After we wash the marks off the wall, I'm going to take the crayons away for a while. Thank you for being truthful."

★ "I'm going to take the crayons away for a few days. But I'm so pleased about your telling me the truth that I'd like to read you a story after we wash off the wall."

There is no attempt here to confuse the two issues. The parent is happy about the truth, but firm in carrying out the consequences of crayon misuse. The truth is rewarded in a way unrelated to the crayon incident. The parent might also choose to react in a more nondirect way.

★ "Thank you for telling me the truth. It helps. Now, if you were the parent, what would you do about the unacceptable use of crayons?"

★ "I'm glad you told me the truth. That's very important. Now, we have a serious problem about the crayons. How can we solve it?"

There will also be many instances when we choose to reward truth by refraining from punishment. We must first decide where we place truth on our scale of values. If it ranks high, we must then be willing to shrug off occasional misdemeanors or at least compromise our penalties to reinforce the child's own valuation of honesty.

Kid Kover-Ups

Nothing is more enchanting than a child's imagination—from an array of pretend friends to a saga of tall tales. Most parents are charmed as they watch their child's fantasies unfold. At the same time they must perform the difficult task of helping the child distinguish between reality and fantasy without inhibiting his gift of imagination. This is particularly important when tales are used to modify facts.

★ "A big purple dinosaur with red glasses came into the living room and knocked over your plant."

★ "I put my bike away, but Batman had to get it out again to chase some bad guys."

★ "At night my doll with the blue dress climbs off the shelf and goes into the bathroom to get me water. Sometimes she spills it."

★ "Tommy is crying because the elephant scared him. It was so big with three green eyes, wings, and a red hat."

One parent calls these tales creative excuses. He answers, "Really? That's a good one. Let me write that down. Three green eyes! That's very creative."

Thus, without undermining the child's imagination, the parent is saying that he is amused but not fooled. The child is reminded that, while it is a lovely story, we know it is just a story.

What if the child is insistent about her version of the story? There are other ways we can humor her imagination but get the message across. With a knowing glint in his eye the parent can say:

★ "Well, I'm going to leave the room for a minute. When I get back, I will expect you and the dinosaur to have picked up the plant. Then I'll help you sweep."

★ "I expect your bike to be put away. Since I don't see Batman around anywhere, I guess it's going to be your responsibility."

★ "Since your doll seems to have stopped walking now, I guess it's up to you to clean up the mess. It's a shame your doll is so quiet. I was planning to give her a glass of juice for being truthful about the mess."

★ "I see only you in the room. Are you sure the elephant wasn't in your mind? When we're sorry about something we've done, we often wish someone else had done it!"

Often a child uses fantasy to fulfill wishes. Although there is no harm done, we can react in a way that further highlights the difference between what is real and what is not.

Ann: I dived off the diving board today at the pool.
Parent: (Knowing Ann is afraid of the deep water) You did? Are you sure?
Ann: Yeah. I dived off.
Parent: I know how much you want to learn to dive in the deep water. Do you think maybe you are telling me what you wish you had done rather than what you did?

Ann: (Reflecting) Yeah. I dived off in my mind.

Parent: I understand. But I know it won't be long before you learn to dive with your body, too.

Ann: Yeah. Pretty soon.

Because fibbing can become an automatic response to many situations, parents need to stress again and again the value of truthfulness.

★ "Telling the truth means a lot to me. Then I can work with the problem as it really is, not as it might be."

★ "Telling the truth is solving a problem in a grown-up way."

★ "It helps when we tell the truth. Then we know exactly where we stand."

Children aren't born George Washingtons. They need lots of practice. What about the examples we set as parents? In one fell swoop we can destroy months of work if we betray our child's trust by breaking our word. Promises must be honored. Our word must be good. If we're going to be gone for the whole day, we don't tell a crying youngster we'll be back in a few minutes. If the child is in the car when we ram the rear of another, we don't let him hear us tell our spouse it was the other driver's fault. We don't say the park is closed when we just don't feel like going; we may see twenty children there when we pass by later.

Authenticity is not always the way of the world, but it surely can be the rule of the home.

What's That You're Hiding in Your Pocket?

If we agree the word *lie* is too strong to attribute to a preschooler, then certainly the word *steal* is formidable. Yet some parents do report that around age three or four, children occasionally come home with items that belong to friends, nursery schools, and grocery stores. Parents are often distressed and always a bit embarrassed by this. But hopefully we don't harbor thoughts that we have a future resident of the state penitentiary on our hands. In fact, the parents who suggested the following methods find that this particular stage in the child's development is usually very short-lived.

As with fibbing, the problem is twofold. First, we must establish the truth about how an item came into the child's possession. Second, we must deal with the issue of not taking things that don't belong to us.

Andy returns home from playgroup with Eddie's favorite car in his pocket.

Parent: I see you have Eddie's car.

Andy: It's mine. He gave it to me.

Parent: You know how important the truth is to me. Now think real hard. Maybe you wanted Eddie to give you the car so much that you pretended he did.

Andy: Yeah. I pretended.

Parent: I understand how much you must have wanted the car. It's very pretty. But it's unacceptable to take things that belong to other people. Eddie is probably real sad about not having his car. I'm glad you told me the truth. It helps. Now we can decide what to do. What do you think we should do?

Andy: Take it back?

Parent: I agree. Want me to go with you?

Child returns home from school with school crayons.

Parent: I see you have crayons that belong to the school.

Child: The teacher said I could bring them home.

Parent: We have crayons. These belong to the school.

Child: They're mine! The teacher said so!

Parent: I want to talk about things like they really are and not how you would like them to be.

Child: I want the crayons!

Parent: I understand you do. They're very nice. But if all children brought crayons home from school, what would you use to color with at school?

Child: They'd be gone.

Parent: That wouldn't be very good, would it?

Child: No.

Parent: What would you like to tell me about the crayons?

Child: The teacher didn't give them to me.

Parent: Thank you for being truthful. Now it's easier for us to talk about what we should do. What do you think we should do?

Nursery school teachers and day-care personnel are seasoned and will usually react in a way that demonstrates the seriousness of the situation while still stressing understanding and forgiveness. If they don't, some dialogue between parent and teacher is called for (or a new nursery school or day-care facility might be considered). Other parents, too, are usually friendly and helpful; they will not condone the act, but they will generally be kind and sympathetic.

What about grocery stores or shop managers? Returning a filched item to a store can be a more difficult matter. We don't want a jolly Santa Claus type to hug the child and say, "What a fine young man to tell the truth! Don't worry about it. In fact, why don't you just keep the gum. Here's a lollipop too."

On the other hand, we don't want to run into a Scrooge who screams, "You little thief! You want to end up in jail?"

Many stores have an established ritual for discussing the problem with youngsters that strikes a happy medium between condemnation and total pardon. If there is no established procedure, it might be helpful to phone the store manager and explain that you are bringing your child in to return an item. By telling the manager a little bit about the child's personality and sensitivities and perhaps offering suggestions, the parent can help the manager handle the situation constructively. The parent should always accompany the child to provide support (and money, if the gum has already been chewed).

And let's not make these return ventures (whether to

store, school, or friends) traumatic experiences. It is better to go through it a dozen times in a peaceful, undramatic way and let the child learn through repetition. Forget adamant nip-this-in-the-bud attitudes.

The habit of not taking things that don't belong to us can also be reinforced in other ways. For example, unless a toy is presented to a child as an official gift, he should not be allowed to take it home with him. Avoid letting small children leave friends' homes with borrowed toys (even if it takes a little longer or is a little harder to make a graceful exit).

★ "It's nice of Ms. James to offer to let you take that home. But why don't we leave it here? Then next time we come you can play with it again."

★ "Thank you, Ms. James, for offering to let Amy take that puzzle. But I think we'd best leave it here. Can you save it for her to play with the next time she comes?"

★ "Amy, why don't you put the puzzle away so you'll know exactly where to find it the next time we come."

In stores, children can be allowed to pay for treats they receive. This shows them that we must account for the things we walk out with. "Here's a quarter. You must give it to the cashier. When you do, the gum will belong to you and you may open it."

Frequent reminders can be given about how purchases are made.

★ "Please put the cookies back on the shelf. We only pick up what we're planning to pay for. Cookies are not on my list of things to buy today."

★ "You may look at all the gum but take only one pack. We are only planning to pay for one."

★ "Please put the socks on the counter until I pay the cashier. Then you may hold them."

★ "Now the bananas belong to us! Would you like to carry them for me?"

With very young children, we need to remember how often they see us leaving stores with sacks full of goodies. The sooner we can acquaint them with how we got those goodies, the sooner they will understand the importance of the proper transaction. Unless, as in the case that follows, your child is ultraperceptive. Five-year-old Mark returned home from a shopping trip during which he had gotten a new pair of shoes. "Aren't you going to wear your new shoes?" his father asked. "I can't wear them yet," answered Mark. "You charged them."

The Kids Versus Ma Bell

It was over sixty years ago that the physiologist Pavlov discovered that dogs could be trained to salivate to a ringing bell once they began to associate the sound of the bell with being fed. Today, parents everywhere claim similar results from children in response to the sound of a ringing telephone.

"At the mere sound of the telephone ringing, Brian drops whatever he is doing and rushes headlong for the refrigerator," confesses one mother.

Another said, "Nancy and Bill start an argument as soon as I pick up the receiver."

"It's somewhat understandable when my three-year-old misbehaves," says a third. "To him the ten minutes I might spend talking on the phone probably seems like an eternity. But how can I explain it when my five-year-old acts even worse? Why does he always pick *that* time to bring the gang in for a snack and then throw a tantrum when I tell him to wait a few minutes until I'm finished?"

The Competitive Spirit

Whether children are six months or six years old, the sight of a parent talking on the telephone seems to bring out their competitive spirit. They *know*, almost instinctively, that at that point Mom or Dad would rather concentrate on that telephone call than on them. So, they proceed to use every means at their disposal to be sure that they aren't ignored during the time the parent is trying to talk. The exact tactics vary, depending on a child's age, but may include crying, yelling, pantomime (clutching the stomach to show that starvation will occur unless sustenance is given immediately), direct action (experimenting with the lipstick found while rummaging in Mom's purse), or various combinations of these.

Parents are not without their own set of conditioned responses. Some have cordless phones or long phone cords so they can retreat into a nearby bathroom or closet and shut the door. Others give asides ("Just a minute, Peter, I'll be right there."), write quick notes, or attempt to fill requests for snacks with the phone tucked securely between ear and shoulder.

These actions may permit a parent to complete that particular phone call and should not be abandoned. Of course, later Dad may realize that he accidentally agreed to supervise the Cub Scout picnic when he was actually saying yes to Todd's request for a glass of water, but that isn't too catastrophic. The question is what might happen next time. The children have been told—for years!—not to misbehave during telephone conversations. Why then does the problem persist?

Our investigations into this area have led us to only one conclusion: that, unfortunately, there doesn't seem to be one definitive answer. Instead, parents appear to cope with telephone antics much as they cope with the common cold; they try many remedies, all of which provide, at best, only temporary relief. However, we believe that "temporary relief" is better than unmitigated suffering. Besides, there is always the hope that further investigations will eventually produce a cure.

Despite this limitation we feel that the problem is worth analyzing because, for most of us, using the telephone is an integral part of daily living. We make phone calls to conduct business, request information, do our shopping, and keep in touch with friends. The telephone allows us to conduct our affairs using less time and energy than would otherwise be possible.

Telephone Time

We are involved with both outgoing and incoming calls. We can exercise some control over outgoing calls. For instance, these calls often can be made while children are napping or in school or occupied elsewhere. Of course, there is no guarantee that the child won't awaken from his nap the minute you begin dialing. And it is true that some calls must be made when children are around— after school, evenings, weekends, *all* summer—but parents can often coordinate their telephone time with periods of relative calm in the household.

The situation changes dramatically, however, with incoming calls. How often have you left word for someone to return a call only to have the phone ring while you are changing the baby's diapers? Or the boss, who hates to bother you at home, picks the moment when the kids are arguing to call with an important message?

It was once predicted that every home would someday be equipped with a picture phone—so you can see people as well as talk to them. Imagine the reaction of your new client as he watches you wrestle the sugar bowl away from little Julie, pour drinks for Amy and her friends, then rescue the refrigerator egg tray that Jeff discovered while your back was turned—all the while discussing plans for a new contract in what (you hope) comes across in a calm, rational manner. Indeed, some ideas are better left off the mass market.

Because we have little control over the timing and nature of incoming calls, we try to borrow the Boy Scout motto and "be prepared." Initially, that means educating children regarding the telephone and our expectation of them while we use it. Naturally, what we expect of toddlers differs from what we expect of school-age children.

With babies and toddlers, prevention is the best answer. These youngsters already know that when you are on the phone they have competition for your attention. To get their share some may whine or pester you for snacks, while others will use this opportunity to explore forbidden areas. Fortunately children at this age are easily distracted. It can help to have a supply of toys somewhere near the phone. These could be special toys that are handed out only when Mom or Dad is on the phone. To include a few snack crackers may be tempting, but remember Pavlov's theory. The link between the ring of the telephone and the crackers in the cupboard seems to be established almost instantaneously.

What Is This Thing Anyway?

Even with very young children, an explanation of what a telephone is and how it works helps. (This should be repeated in greater detail at intervals as the child matures.) Consider the scene from the child's point of view. There you are, totally engrossed with a plastic apparatus clamped tightly to your ear. Sometimes you are talking to it, but it doesn't appear to answer. Sometimes you appear to be listening, but there is no indication of what you might be listening to. Certainly to a small child it must be very difficult to understand why his noise would constitute an interruption of this meaningless-looking activity.

Often, we forget to explain the obvious. We need to help the child understand that there is another person involved in this activity. You can continue your description with, "Grandma is in her house talking into her telephone, just as I am doing here. When Grandma talks I have to be quiet so I can hear what she is saying. Then she is quiet while I talk to her." When it is appropriate, let the child listen to hear the voice in the receiver. He probably won't talk into the phone yet, but the experience reinforces the concept you are trying to present. Later on the more complicated aspects of the telephone, such as the voice waves being sent across telephone lines, can be added to further instruct curious minds. Also, the idea of concentrating on the telephone out of respect for the caller can be introduced. "When you make noise, it is hard for me to hear what Grandma is saying to me."

A Time for Compromise

At this age, as with children of all ages, parents must be reasonable about the length of time they spend on a particular call. Although you might wish to chat at length with Cousin Alice, trying to do so near your child's naptime or a mealtime probably will mean pushing too far.

To avoid problems, ordinarily keep calls as short as possible, indulging in gab sessions only as circumstances permit. This is not to say that parents should allow children to control their use of the telephone. Parents certainly have the right to use the phone and should be able to expect acceptable behavior from their children while they do so. Still, fair expectations must consider a child's patience threshold at a particular age.

Preschoolers are definitely capable of understanding more than their younger siblings. They are also capable of being more disruptive if they choose to be. Education regarding expectations then must become more explicit. "When I am talking on the telephone, I expect you to play quietly."

The "Just a Minute" Technique

Sometimes children relax if they realize that you will remain occupied only for a limited amount of time. "I must talk to Mr. Welch for five more minutes," or "I will be finished by the time you color that picture."

A reminder of what you wish might be helpful. "I really must talk to this man right now. I expect you to show good manners so we can finish this conversation."

A promise of things to come may work wonders. "After I finish this call, I will fix you a snack." Then you do, as soon as you put the receiver down.

The "Say Hi to Grandma" Technique

Some children are upset by being excluded from participating in the use of the telephone. If the caller is a friend or relative, a few seconds of letting Jenny talk—saying "bye-bye" as she finishes—may be enough. Naturally this technique will not work if the caller is your insurance agent or if Jenny usually doesn't abide by her short good-bye; however, it works with some children and is probably worth trying.

The "Good Job" Technique

When children react as you want them to, use positive reinforcement. Simple statements such as, "Thank you very much for not disturbing me during that call," further help children understand what you expect of them. If possible, continue with something like, "In fact, I feel so good that I'd like to read a story to you now," or "That was an important phone call, and your cooperation leaves me some extra time here. Why don't we do a puzzle?"

When Your Child Is More Important than the Phone

At times children may feel as though the telephone has a higher priority in the household than they do. Perhaps Dad has just settled down to play a game with them when—whoops!—there goes that telephone and off goes Dad, game forgotten. Think how good a child would feel if once in a while Dad answered that phone and quickly excused himself, saying, "Let me call you back later. I've just started playing 'Candy Land' with Lynn and we'd like to finish."

Some parents may even be able to refrain from jumping up and running every time the phone rings saying, "I think I'd rather finish reading this story to you." If you feel you must answer the phone and you cannot call back, try to finish quickly, letting the child know that it is because you would rather play with him that you cut the call short.

These days, there are plenty of devices to give you control over how much the telephone controls you. For starters, you can monitor your calls with the use of an answering machine. If you want the house quiet during naptime, you can simply turn off the ringer and turn the volume down on the answering machine, so that the messages are recorded soundlessly. The phone-mail systems available now offer very efficient methods of answering calls and saving messages. Of course, these techniques may be impractical if you are trying to run a business from your home, and you feel that you must answer all calls when they come in. In that case, you might consider a system called a "piggyback" line. This is a second phone number, but it comes into your home on the same line. Using this, you would maintain one number as your personal home phone number, and a second number for business and customers. Each number has its own distinct ring, so that when a call comes into your house, the sound of the ring will tell you if it is a personal call or a business one.

When It Doesn't Work

And what if, despite all your preparations and positive reinforcement, children fail to meet your carefully explained expectations? Then you can certainly show your displeasure, "I am very angry. I know that you can behave better than you did while I was trying to talk to Reverend Smith," and proceed to discipline in ways appropriate to the age of the child and consistent with policies generally followed in the household.

Unfortunately, as we said at the beginning of this chapter, children of all ages have a difficult time learning—

and remembering—how to act when Mom and Dad are using the telephone. Constant reminders seem to be the rule rather than the exception, that is, progress comes slowly. And it takes just one child feeling ornery to revert back to former intrusive behavior. Perhaps by revising expectations, planning our calls, and adopting a more flexible attitude when we are interrupted, we can improve the quality of our telephone time. That is probably the best that most of us can hope for!

"But Big Bird Is My *Best* Friend!"

Scene: Bedtime.

Parent: Come on. Time for bed.

Kids: Just five more minutes. This is the best part of the show.

Scene: Later.

Parent: Now your show is over. Let's go upstairs.

Kids: Oh, come on. We've been waiting *all week* for this show. Can't we stay up a little later? PLEASE?!!

Scene: The sandbox. Lynn, age two-and-a-half, and Tara, age three, are playing.

Lynn: I make cookies.

Tara: And I eat them up like Cookie Monster—chomp! chomp!

Lynn: I watch Bert and Ernie on TV.

Tara: Me, too.

Lynn: And Big Bird is my best friend.

Tara: Mine, too.

> *Scene:* The car. Dad and Mark, age four, are driving past a local shopping center.
>
> *Mark:* Hey, Dad, there's Sears.
>
> *Dad:* How can you tell?
>
> *Mark:* I can read it. See, s-e-a . . . r-s. I learned that on TV.

Television. No matter what our feelings are toward it, it is a part of our lives. But how can we take advantage of its good points without succumbing to all the horrors we read and hear about?

Chances are you already share the beliefs of many parents that

★ The amount of time spent watching TV should be carefully limited, and

★ The programs a child watches should be carefully monitored.

But how do we implement these decisions? How much TV is too much? Who will control the TV set? Can children be taught to use TV wisely even when we are not looking over their shoulders?

In the Beginning . . .

It starts off relatively simply. You have one child, age eighteen months, whom you occasionally plop in front of "Mister Rogers" while you rush around doing daily chores. The baby doesn't realize that anything different may be on another station; and, besides, she likes the way he ties his sneakers. So, for an hour she may sit and watch TV or alternate between the show and her toys. After the show, you appear and flick the off switch, and the kindly Fred Rogers disappears. (Does he live inside there? The baby may wonder.) And now baby is ready to amuse herself or be amused until the magic box brings another friend around.

Later . . .

Children may not go along with your ideas quite readily. By the time they begin preschool (earlier if they are not the oldest child in the family), they begin to develop definite preferences for certain shows. Even though it was a parental favorite, one little boy we know refused to watch "Mister Rogers." Every time the show was turned on he would watch it for two minutes, then say, "Good-bye, Mr. Rogers," and turn the channel.

In addition to choosing shows, preschoolers start to want the TV on when they decide it should be on. They may argue that the one hour in the morning should be stretched to two or that the afternoon shows start a little earlier. When parents say no, the preschoolers get very upset.

About this time television commercials begin to exert their influence. You may first notice this when you take the children to the grocery store and find that they begin asking for every kind of junk cereal on the shelves. Or you find that they have absorbed messages aimed at adults. Then you are apt to hear that you must buy Downy or you can't do the laundry properly. One parent said that if her children were playing in a room in which television was on for the adults, they would interrupt their play *only* for the commercials. At those times their complete attention would be riveted toward the television set. (Many commercials are more colorful and louder than the regular programming.)

This is the time to start to counteract the daily influence of television. One can begin by explaining the house rules for TV watching. Simple rules adhered to when children are young can prevent more serious arguments later.

House Rules for TV Watching

Watch Only Your Shows Not all TV shows are meant for family viewing. Some are strictly for grown-ups. Others might be okay for adults and big brother Mike. Still others are *especially* for *you*.

Try to Watch Grow Shows and Avoid Too Many Junk Shows Borrowing these terms from our nutrition chapter, we apply them to TV. "Grow" shows are shows that feed our brains. "Junk" shows are those that leave us starving. While some fall clearly into one category or the other, many fall somewhere in between. Children can become quite sophisticated at determining a show's merits. Even four-year-olds begin to recognize that certain shows are mostly junk or half grow, half junk. By kindergarten some can rationalize that, "Yes, this show is junk, but it's Saturday morning and I've been growing all week and now it's time for a little junk, okay?" (Because Saturday morning is often the time for adults to get caught up on sleep, many parents might concede the point.)

Doing Is Better than Watching Although there are many things to be learned from television shows, all the information is transmitted via one-way communication. Children still need to gain most of their knowledge actively, by talking, manipulating materials, participating in gross motor activities, or interacting with groups of people. Statements such as, "I like to see you playing with your dolls," or "Playing outside with your tricycle gives you lots of exercise," help preschoolers understand how important it is for them to *do* things.

There Are Only Certain Times We Watch TV The exact times will vary depending on families' schedules, preferences, and local offerings. Some popular choices include: mornings, to wake up gradually, lunchtime, late afternoon, and early evening. Some parents believe that television is relaxing to a child. This may or may not be the case, and certainly depends on the type of program.

When Friends Come Over to Play, TV Goes Off The key word here is *play*. When children get together, they usually prefer to be active. Most children will understand when it is explained that, "In our house we don't watch TV when our friends are here. Let Brian show you where he keeps his toys."

Note to Parents The best way to demonstrate these rules to children is by your example. Children are very quick to notice any discrepancies between what you say and what you do. For instance, you make them choose their shows and then limit the hours during which TV is on for them. But do you turn the set on at 7:00 P.M. for yourself and keep it on until 11:00, watching whatever happens to be there? Or, even worse, do you use it as background noise while trying to talk to friends who have dropped by? When television is on do children have to compete with it for your attention? If you expect children to use—not abuse—the TV set, are you willing to shut it off unless one of *your* shows is on? Can we relearn the art of conversation among family members? Are we willing to read *Cinderella* to our child rather than yelling at her to be quiet while "Monday Night Football" is on? Does the TV set appear to have a higher priority in the household than the people? Parents must be willing to set the example if they expect children to follow suit.

Note for Baby-Sitters Nothing can undermine the house rules faster than a baby-sitter who introduces the children to the joys of uninterrupted television viewing, completely disregarding the content of the shows. Thus, each sitter should be aware of the restrictions you observe regarding use of the television set. A simple instruction should be enough, such as, "John and Maria are only allowed to watch Channel 11 for one hour after school. Then please have them play outside or with their games."

"But without television, what will I do with him all day long, especially in the winter?" moaned one parent. That is a valid point for many of us who may have begun to think of television as a baby-sitter. We can't entertain youngsters all day. But we can—and should—help children learn to entertain themselves.

★ Keep toys within a child's reach.

★ Have an adequate supply of arts and crafts materials that the child can use with a minimum of supervision, for which the ground rules have already been established.

★ Recognize your child's need to have friends over to play occasionally.

And Later Still . . .

We have the more sophisticated child—the TV veteran. Although most of what we have already said still applies, some things definitely change at this point. For instance, Julie is no longer dependent on you to manipulate the dials on the TV set. In fact, many four- and five-year-olds have a better command of this process than their parents. Also, she may have a thorough knowledge of the *TV Guide*, gleaned from her own TV watching and with any blanks cheerfully filled in by helpful peers. Arguments in favor of watching this or that particular show may grow more emotional, "But I *have* to watch 'ER' tonight. Kristen and Ann are going to. I'm not a baby any more you know."

Now instead of dictating the terms for TV watching, it may be better to include children in the decision-making process. For instance, it may be time to begin letting them decide when they would like to watch TV, staying within acceptable parameters. One little boy we know became very adept at scheduling his TV viewing time. Knowing that he was allowed two hours on Saturday morning (a house rule), he chose to watch from 8:00 A.M. to 9:00 A.M. Then he shut the set off for half an hour and resumed watching from 9:30 to 10:30. But there was still a half hour show he wanted to watch. So he bargained with his father that, if allowed to watch another thirty minutes, he would forego watching any more TV later in the day. That meant no movies in the evening, but he knew this and made his decision accordingly.

Parents still have an obligation to tune in to the quality of shows watched by older children; again, bring them into the decision. Talk about the show. Have the child describe what she likes about it. Give your opinion. Be candid while being careful not to put the child down for expressing what she thinks. After all, many networks strive to be uncomplicated; they may have just what it takes to appeal to a four- or five-year-old. Think a minute. If you were a kid, wouldn't you like all those car chases and slapstick jokes?

When shows are clearly objectionable, be they too adult or just plain tasteless, the channel should be changed or the set turned off. Explain what you are doing and why, "This show is for adults. Right now you proba- bly wouldn't like it or would misunderstand it. Don't worry, there will be something on for you later," or "This show is terrible and the only way we can let those who produced it know what we think is by shutting it off."

Most newer television sets are equipped with parental control features that allow you to completely lock out cer- tain channels. You can choose which networks you con- sider objectionable and rig the television so that these channels cannot be tuned in. This works well for our young channel surfers as well as baby-sitters who might decide to ignore our rules. You can also block the set from being used for video games, if you wish. If your tele- vision set is not equipped with channel locks, you may be able to rent a cable box equipped with parental con- trols from your cable company.

There is one final concept to consider, and it applies to all our TV rules—flexibility. Once control over the TV set has been clearly established, rules can be adjusted to fit circumstances without dire consequences. For instance, time limits may be changed when there is a rainy day or when a child or parent is ill. Or friends can be invited in to watch a rented movie after school.

Videocassette recorders make it possible to record or rent the good television shows and children's movies and have them available for viewing at times compatible with the family schedule.

Some TV is good. Most of it is mediocre or just plain bad. But it is here to stay and it is part of our daily lives. One of the best things we can do for our children is to teach them to be intelligent TV consumers.

Take Me Along

Scene: The grocery store, Saturday morning. Dad and the kids arrive to do the weekly shopping. Brian, age two, is immediately deposited in a cart, while four-year-old Lisa is allowed to walk.

Dad: (Getting out the list) Lisa, you stay right next to this cart and make sure Brian doesn't throw anything out.

Scene: Ten minutes later. Lisa has disappeared. Dad and Brian are stopped in front of the sugar, where Dad is preoccupied deciding which brand is the better buy.

Brian: (Turning around in his seat, grabs for the egg carton) Mine!

Dad: (Quickly looks up and reaches to slap his hand) Don't touch that!

Brian: (Begins to scream)

Lisa: (Returns, carrying with her a packaged doll) I want this.

Dad: (Still holding sugar and moving eggs to a safer spot) I told you not to ask for anything. Now go put that back!

Lisa: But I want it!

Dad: I said NO!

Lisa: (Starts to cry and run)

Dad: (Drops the sugar he's been holding into the cart and goes after her) Come back here!

Brian: (Stops screaming to reach for the sugar)

Scene: When Dad returns, with a loudly protesting Lisa, he finds Brian mesmerized by the white crystals as they flow from the sugar bag to the floor.

Another scene takes place on a Friday night. The family has planned to go out to dinner and decides to try a new restaurant that the newspaper claims has excellent prime rib. Both parents are tired, having followed hectic schedules all week. The children, Emily, age four, and Tracy, age two, have enjoyed an afternoon of vigorous play at the park and appear more interested in who's going to win the battle over a toy fire engine than going out to dinner.

A short ride later (and after a heated debate involving "who's going to sit where"), the family arrives at its destination. A quick glance at the parking lot tells them that everyone else in town read the same glowing review. Dad suggests going somewhere else, but Mom insists that she's been planning on eating here and a short wait won't matter.

Forty-five minutes later, the family is shown to a table. Emily's dress sports a soggy stain where Tracy bumped into her, causing her to spill her Coke. Tracy's eyelids are beginning to close and the sleepier she grows, the more fidgety and cranky she becomes.

A glance at the menu does little to improve things. At the top of the page is a note: "For all dinners, allow thirty minutes." Also, there is no children's menu, and Emily is loudly announcing that she wants a McDonald's hamburger and a milk shake. Tracy says she wants to go home and begins to cry. When last heard, Mom was hissing through clenched teeth, "Now sit still and stop crying or I'll really give you something to cry about."

Most of us with preschoolers have at one time or another been in situations similar to these. We have inwardly vowed never to take these kids out in public again. However, we may be able to keep this promise only until we have to go to the store again, or head for the doctor's office, or remember that we're supposed to take the children to the family picnic at Aunt Margaret's next Sunday. Let's face it, American families with young children are on the go now as never before, and hiring baby-sitters all the time not only would be extremely expensive, but would rob the children (and parents!) of many opportunities to enjoy life together as a family. Rather than issuing vague threats that we really can't or don't want to carry out, our goal should be to learn from past mistakes so that future excursions can be more beneficial and pleasant for everyone.

"Great idea," you agree, "but you've never seen my three boys in action. The last time we took them to the movies, between trips to the concession stand and to the bathroom and crying over spilt popcorn or who hit whom—well, I don't think any of us watched more than five minutes of the show. Maybe when the baby is six we'll try again, but not before."

We admit that there are problems involved when young children accompany parents to public places. But we also believe that an understanding of the situation combined with careful preplanning will help minimize these difficulties. What follows are some ideas for doing that.

The Destination

Family outings can be roughly divided into three main groups.

Necessary

There are some places where you must take the children at one time or another. For most people these include doctors' and dentists' offices, grocery stores, and other stores (periodically it *is* necessary to measure Eric's foot before buying new shoes).

Probably Necessary

You and your family could physically survive if you never took long trips by car or plane to visit Grandma, or never took the children with you to church, or never let them go to birthday parties. But how do you explain to Grandma that, once again, you won't be able to visit because you can't face six (or sixteen) hours in the car with Jennifer and Todd? Or how do you explain that Julie is the only kindergartner who has never been to a birthday party?

Optional

Optional outings are those that truly broaden a child's experience and can provide chances for all members of the family to thoroughly enjoy themselves. Included here are outings to restaurants, movies, the zoo, the circus, the local fire station, a nearby farm, or the aquarium. These outings can be eliminated if children and parents honestly can't cope with them, but life is immeasurably richer for those who choose to partake in them.

Having decided that as mature, capable adults we certainly can handle all three types of outings, we can look for some common threads underlying all outings.

Basic Ground Rules

Fair Expectations

Make sure you don't plan outings that by their very nature ask more of the child than his age and maturity level allow him to handle. For instance, expecting a preschooler to stand in long lines for a special museum exhibit is probably not the best way to introduce him to the wonders of abstract art or the treasures of Egypt. Neither is it fair to expect our resident live wires to amuse themselves on a lengthy car trip by gazing quietly out the window, absorbing the scenic wonders that normally border interstate highways.

Advance Preparation

For outings you deem appropriate, prepare the child for what probably will occur and what type of behavior you expect. Not every three-year-old instinctively knows the proper etiquette to be followed when he is a guest at a birthday party. Most of us can give adequate explanations about what to expect at birthday parties or choose appropriate children's books to help illustrate our points. We know one mother who went a step further and engaged in role-playing with her daughter. Together they went through taking turns for games, learning the words to "Happy Birthday," letting the birthday boy open his gifts and blow out his own candles, and using a fork while eating birthday cake. The little girl went confidently off to the party, well-prepared for almost anything that might happen.

Children learn very early that different rules apply in different homes or in different situations. Visiting relatives might be more enjoyable if the child is told in advance that "even though we sometimes eat with our fingers at home, at Grandma's she expects you to use a fork or spoon," or "In our house we sometimes run, but at Aunt Catherine's we only walk." Many children are pleased to be taken into an adult's confidence and are proud of themselves when they live up to our realistic expectations.

Heed the Needs of the Youngest Child

This is an extension of fair expectations, but it's worth emphasizing. If this outing is for the enjoyment of the entire family, make sure you consider the needs of *everyone*. No matter how much the rest of the family may want to spend the afternoon at the hockey game, the ability of everyone to enjoy the game will largely depend upon the contentment of two-year-old Daniel. If it's not likely that he can sit through a four-hour game, it might be better either to get a baby-sitter for him or to choose another destination. On the other hand, if he is able to sit still for long periods of time and has shown a definite interest in action sports, perhaps he can go along—as long as someone remembers to bring toys to occupy him should his attention lag toward the end.

Pay Attention to the Children

Keep them amused. If you want to dawdle over coffee after dinner, don't plan to take the children that night.

Don't Worry About Uncle Harry

If you're comfortable with your children's behavior, relax and enjoy yourself, despite Uncle Harry's comments about their roughness or lack of manners or how much better behaved children *used* to be. Maybe the ones he remembers were eight instead of three, or maybe his memory isn't too accurate.

Positive Reinforcement

Always reward successful outings with plenty of sincere, positive reinforcement. "This worked out so well, I want to do it again!"

Despite these general rules, many parents still feel apprehensive about taking their children on outings. "Just thinking about taking Joey to the doctor puts a knot in my stomach," confessed one mother, "and I'm sure that my uptightness contributes to what always turns out to be total disaster."

This mother then went on to say that the main thing that made her nervous was that the doctor was invariably late and she simply couldn't make Joey sit still.

Question: Is it fair to expect a three-year-old to sit still for an hour with nothing more amusing to look at than back issues of *Good Housekeeping*?

To help solve this problem and others like it, we now offer some parent-tested ideas to help other parents plan some of the more common types of family excursions.

Special Tactics for Necessary Trips

The Grocery Store

★ Establish a basic routine that doesn't vary too much. Make sure children know the answers to such concerns as, "One treat?" "Two treats?" or "Don't ask."

★ Keep children confined to a cart as long as possible. Even after they have begun demanding to walk, offer chances to ride. A suprising number of four-year-olds, having established their independence, will not be too proud to get back in the cart.

★ When possible, talk about what you're buying and why. "This week I think we'll buy some chicken because that's your favorite," or "The nice juicy apples will be a special treat for you." Not only will a child be more entertained, but he will also be learning some valuable lessons in vocabulary and nutrition.

★ Let older ones help choose certain things. "We need to get some ice cream. Should we get chocolate or strawberry?"

★ Those who don't ride can also be helpful when it comes to finding some items.

★ If a child tends to grab things off the shelves, either here or in other stores, explain that, "Here we only take things we plan to buy, and I will let you know what we plan to buy."

   Other phrases that help control grabbing wherever it may occur could be, "Use only one finger for touching" (unless that finger is as gentle as a bulldozer), or

"This is a look place, not a touch place," or "We use our eyes here, not our hands."

★ Sometimes the battle of the candy counter can be solved by giving a child a choice among some acceptable items. "Here are your kinds of gum. You may choose either the green or red package." (Naturally, the choices are sugarless varieties.)

Other Shopping Trips

Many children enjoy shopping for a *limited* time, especially if you are shopping for something for them. For others, their displeasure means sheer torture for both of you. Know your own child and his limitations and try to act accordingly. If you have serious shopping to do (clothes for yourself or comparative shopping for a new household item), try to leave the child at home with a sitter or go when he's at nursery school or otherwise engaged. If you must bring him along, keep the following guidelines in mind.

★ Keep the items you're looking for at a minimum and try to accomplish your errands as quickly as possible.

★ Don't go to places that feature predominantly fragile merchandise (unless the thought of bankruptcy doesn't panic you).

★ You can sometimes keep little ones occupied with outlandish requests. One mother sat her two-year-old in front of the store window and told her to watch for trains. A saleslady, overhearing the conversation, gave the mother a strange look and politely said that there were no trains within miles of the shopping center. "Oh, that's okay," the mother replied, "by the time she realizes that, she'll be out of this stage."

★ The promise of a treat after you finish your errands often gives children incentive to help you via good behavior. These treats can be anything that both you and your children decide is pleasurable—enjoying a shopper's lunch in the cafeteria, spending extra time playing near the fountain, viewing seasonal displays, or taking a walk through the pet store.

This treat is possible only if you haven't put severe time pressure on yourself. With shopping (as with so many other things) try to plan ahead so that you leave yourself ample time to accomplish your tasks. Everyone gets caught occasionally, but try to avoid looking for just the right shoes the day of the party.

Doctors' and Dentists' Offices

★ With some children, the mere mention of a visit to the doctor or dentist provokes tantrums and crying scenes, which is not the type of attitude likely to foster a pleasant doctor–patient relationship. The first step is to change the image of these health-care friends. The parent can begin by approaching visits to the doctor or dentist positively. "I'm sorry your throat hurts, but I'm sure that Dr. Smith can give you something to make it feel better." "The dentist makes sure that our teeth stay strong and healthy."

Another source of good information comes from the many fine children's books that explain the function of doctors and dentists. The detailed pictures which often accompany the text help youngsters become familiar with the tools and procedures used during office visits. Knowing what to expect lessens fear of the unknown.

Advance knowledge also applies to such crucial questions as, "Am I going to get a shot?" or "Will she use the drill?" Be honest in your answer. If a shot is even within the realm of possibility, don't rule it out. "I'm not sure he'll need to give you a shot for this but he might. I *am* sure that he'll look in your ears and down your throat and listen to your heart."

★ Never belittle a child for her fear of shots. How many adults are truly blasé about needles? Instead, show that you understand her feelings. "I know that shots don't feel too good, but luckily they only hurt for a minute, and the medicine in the needle will keep you from catching the measles." (Stress the positive, again!) "Don't worry, I'll be right there with you."

★ Having convinced (?) the child that the doctor is indeed her friend, you must now overcome the ordeal of the waiting room—a very appropriately named room considering the schedules followed by many physicians. How do you keep a child from totally destroying your nerves and the medical building during a forty-five minute wait?

Bring along something to do unless your doctor keeps a waiting room stocked with a chalkboard, a fish tank, a laundry basket full of toys, a stack of interesting books, paper and crayons, small trucks, dolls, or even soft balls. Here is an excellent opportunity to bring out those favorite stories that are simply too long to be read at ordinary sittings. And don't be surprised if you notice you've collected an audience after the first few pages. Just hope that the boy breathing down your daughter's neck doesn't have the chicken pox! Small toys can also be carried into the examining room if another wait is likely there.

★ A reward upon leaving the office lets a child know you truly appreciate his efforts to cooperate. Some offices generously offer little presents. Some dentists keep a treasure chest full of inexpensive surprises. If these things aren't available to you, provide your own reward (and don't forget other siblings who were forced to tag along). This ending *almost* makes undergoing the rigors of an office visit worthwhile.

Acceptable Car Behavior

The battle between parents and children over proper car behavior is one that parents must win. It is, quite literally, a matter of life and death. Usually there is little problem in the early years because the child is confined in an infant or toddler seat. The trouble begins when Wendy learns how to get out of this safety device. From then on, it quickly can become a battle of wills to see whether she will remain confined, either with a half-seat or with a regular seat belt if she is mature enough.

Be prepared to deal with strong protests. One mother simply strapped her child in and, amidst the screams of disapproval, told her daughter that the car wouldn't move unless the seat belt remained buckled and the howls ceased. Eventually, the child got tired of sitting in the car in the garage and quieted down.

This technique of stopping the car and not moving can be used when disputes among children threaten your sanity (and safety) while driving. Some parents even keep a book in the car to read while the children settle themselves down. Children quickly learn that you're not bluffing—especially when you'd rather finish the chapter than go to the grocery store anyway—and reaction times speed up. Once order is restored, the trip is resumed.

Outings That Are Probably Necessary

Most families love to plan trips, be they weekend jaunts or longer vacations. The secret is to get the family from home to destination with everyone still on speaking terms. A few suggestions from well-traveled families might help.

Trips by Car

★ Remember to provide *many* things to keep the children amused.

Dole out inexpensive surprise bags en route.

Old familiar favorites induce quiet play.

If you have the equipment, tape some of their favorite records to be played on a portable cassette player. This is effective if you can tolerate fifty renditions of the Cookie Monster singing "C Is for Cookie."

Involve them in games: looking out the window and counting trucks or guessing what might be inside, playing "the first one to see a . . . ," or picking out certain letters of the alphabet on signs.

Plastic window decorations, which usually are sold for holidays, can be stuck to car windows and peeled off innumerable times without leaving a mark.

★ Make frequent R&R stops. Traveling with young children is not the time to try to break any time records. Bring along a ball to encourage running exercise during some stops (and bless the rest areas that provide swings and slides).

★ Provide snacks. If you don't worry about the crumbs, dry cereal, crackers, small cookies, or raisins are welcome treats. A thermos of juice or water also comes in handy between stops.

★ When possible, picnics are ideal for traveling families. Even two-day trips can be planned when the lunch basket includes a loaf of bread, a jar of peanut butter, a can of deviled ham, or a jar of nonrefrigerated cheese.

★ Look ahead only to the next stop. "Soon we'll be stopping for lunch," or "When we stop for gas, we can play ball." Don't expect preschoolers to be patient with "Tomorrow night we'll be at Grandma's so relax until then." To most youngsters, that's equivalent to next week.

Trips by Plane

★ Try to schedule flights at other than peak times. Friday evening should be avoided; Thursday midday could be more pleasurable. Don't count on having your children sleep on late-night flights. In fact, the only passengers wide awake at 12:45 A.M. are often the preschool set.

★ Taking a plane trip can be a special event. Discuss details beforehand to make it more meaningful to a child. Explain the functions of the pilot and copilot, where the baggage is stored, and the duties of the flight attendants.

★ Some youngsters tend to be cranky on an airplane because their ears bother them. You can help alleviate this by having them chew gum, suck candy, or even drink something during takeoff and landing. With babies you can breastfeed or offer a bottle.

★ Although many airlines supply *some* playthings to amuse children, these may be too advanced or otherwise unappealing to some youngsters. Thus, be sure you bring along a good supply of toys and books that can be comfortably used at your seat.

★ Mealtime aboard a plane can be an adventure. Many airlines will provide special kids' meals if you notify them a few days in advance. Because most children prefer hamburgers to the best gourmet delights, this is quite a treat. Just be sure you identify yourself to the flight attendants early in the flight so that they don't inadvertently give the only two burgers on the plane to some other lucky kids. Also, if two parents are traveling together, it's sometimes easier to eat in shifts, with one of you being responsible for attending to the needs of the children. If you are alone and need assistance, ask the flight attendants; most of them will be happy to help you.

★ If the flight is smooth, a walk up and down the aisle might help cure an attack of restlessness. Although some passengers like to sleep or read during a plane trip, many others will be delighted to help amuse a two-year-old for a few minutes.

Visiting Friends and Relatives

The payoff for teaching our children acceptable manners comes when both we and they are able to relax while visiting friends and relatives, confident that we're all welcome guests. This is not to say that disputes among children will never develop or that Mary will never be caught saying something disrespectful, for these things happen occasionally.

A relaxed atmosphere is more likely to occur when the rules of home do not conflict with what is expected at the place being visited. The most likely occasions for wide divergence come when you visit someone of another generation such as a grandparent or great-aunt. Here, perhaps, more formality is called for than you live with day to day. Plan to discuss these differences with your children ahead of time, explaining that "in different homes we sometimes have to follow different rules." Then, bring along enough appropriate toys to keep the children occupied for the duration of your stay. (It is usually better to leave the loud fire engine or the ear-piercing flute at home and bring things that encourage quieter play.)

Protecting Your Host's Home

If a child is too young to have developed proper table manners, try to feed him earlier in the kitchen, rather than develop a migraine during dinner trying to keep his squash from landing on the white dining room rug. And if Grandma hasn't put her antique vases out of the reach of curious hands, tactfully do this yourself. "You know, Mom, I'll relax a lot more if these things are out of reach. Not that Mark would purposely break them, but they're so lovely, and he is so curious about everything new he sees."

Sometimes trying to take children certain places is more trouble than it's worth. For example, would you really enjoy taking your active bull-in-the-china-shop child to visit your friend with the antique glassware collection? This is especially dangerous if your friend has one of those children who never touches anything so she has kept the fragile pieces displayed. It's all right to restrict your visits to "adults only" for the few months it may take your child to outgrow his grabby phase. Even if you never discuss it together, your friend probably will thank you for your courtesy.

During this period, keep stressing proper behavior with your child at home. "Be gentle." "Just look, don't touch." Then, as he outgrows this phase, he will have an acceptable tool to use in place of his former behavior.

Optional Outings

Optional outings should be your most relaxed outings, for you are under no obligation to stay if things go wrong. Sometimes even the best laid plans go awry when a child misses a nap or is otherwise simply out of sorts.

Restaurants

★ In the beginning, choose only those restaurants that welcome families. There you are more apt to find a menu, prices, and an atmosphere suitable for a family outing. If you are unsure about a particular restaurant, call ahead and ask. This saves you from being seated before learning that there's absolutely nothing Jennifer will eat.

★ Even so, remember that this is no place to plan to linger over cocktails or coffee. Most children can be expected to behave for a while (until their hunger has been satisfied). Then it is usually time to leave.

★ Family excursions to restaurants are not a time for adults to plan to enjoy in-depth conversations. Save those for dinners out as a couple. Use this time to enjoy the kids and engage in family discussions.

★ Be sure your children know what is expected of them before you leave home. Must they sit at the table, or will they be allowed to wander? Some parents are comfortable when their children walk around. The decision depends on circumstances. Many adults enjoying a dinner out do not appreciate a visit from the four-year-old from a neighboring table. Children should be taught that at some restaurants, remaining at the table is a must.

★ Many parents bring crayons and paper so that their child may amuse herself while waiting for her food.

★ If a restaurant is particularly quiet, a child may need gentle reminders to use his restaurant voice, so as not to disturb others.

★ Don't worry about nutrition here. Let children order their favorites—even if it turns out to be plain spaghetti, white rolls, milk, and vanilla ice cream.

★ Enlist the aid of the older children to help amuse the younger ones. Some children are very proud to be entrusted with this responsibility. Also, older ones can pay the check—another ploy that allows them to feel grown up.

Special Places

★ Once again, if possible, prepare the child in advance for what he will be seeing. Not only will it help prepare him for the appropriate kind of behavior, but more importantly, he will more fully understand and appreciate the entertainment. How much more enjoyable the movie *Pocahontas* is if a child is familiar with the story. And a museum exhibit about Native Americans can capture the full attention of any three-year-old who loves action stories.

★ If it is likely that the lights will be dimmed during your outing—for example, at the movies, or circus, or an ice show—or if anything else unusual might occur, tell the children in advance. Put your arm around a little one or even let him sit on your lap if that will comfort him. Once the initial shock wears off, he will probably willingly return to his own seat.

★ Many special attractions for families peddle junk foods and souvenirs very heavily. Decide in advance what your policy is and explain it to your children. "I don't have money for popcorn," or "You may choose one treat or souvenir and that is all." Whatever your policy, be consistent at most events, and they will come to expect that and no more.

★ Too much of a good thing is wearing, even for adults. Be prepared to stay only as long as the children can take it. Nowhere is it written that you have to see the whole museum. If you're visiting a zoo or any place that requires a lot of walking, remember that little legs tire quickly. See the most important things, such as the Children's Zoo, first; anything else is a bonus. Of course, sometimes even four-year-olds can be persuaded to use a stroller—especially if you are able to point out a lot of other big kids who are also enjoying this easier means of transportation.

Outings that go well are the fringe benefits of family life. The best part of sharing our world with our children is getting to see how it looks through their brand-new eyes.

Bedtime Stories

A Fairy Tale

Parents of toddlers still surrounded by the retaining walls of cribs may ask, "What's the big deal about getting a child to bed?" Most likely, it is their cherished belief that when bedtime arrives, they simply transport the child to the bedroom; perform the necessary cleanup; deposit her under the blankets; make sure all stuffed animals are in their usual places; dole out hugs, kisses, and pats on the head; whisper good night; and leave the room in full confidence that, excepting dire emergencies, the next parent–child contact will occur the following morning. And they live happily ever after.

We used to believe in fairy tale endings, too. That was until our children outgrew their cribs and found that physical freedom, when combined with the wonders of growing older and smarter, created previously unimaginable possibilities for extending the day. How wonderful that a few inches of body length and the introduction of a new sleeping apparatus could result in a challenge worthy of a child's best efforts. Bed is escapable; you just have to play your cards right.

"So, okay," parents may retort, "the child is no longer physically prevented from leaving her bed. What's the worst that could possibly happen?" That is an interesting question.

The Late, Late Show

Taking, for the sake of simplicity, one two-and-a-half-year-old and two previously unsuspecting parents, here is what *could* possibly happen. It is 11:00 P.M. Melissa was originally taken to bed at 8:00 P.M. Behold, here she is three hours later enjoying David Letterman with Mom and Dad. Actually, she is the only one enjoying it. While Melissa is laughing and jumping and dancing and skipping, Dad is slouched on the couch, eyes glazed over, worn out from the physical exertions of carrying Melissa back to bed ten—make that eleven—times. Mom, on the other hand, is wide awake. Frustration has a way of keeping mind and body revved up at the end of a long day.

Nevertheless, they are trying to be humane parents. They are trying desperately to understand how Melissa could be displaying three times the energy they have between them. Yet, here she is asserting, "not sleepy," and all indications certainly point to that conclusion. Her behavior shows no signs of that grouchiness that might suggest a need to sleep. On the contrary, with abundant smiles and kisses, cute little prances and leaps, she has rarely been more delightful. Why, they ask themselves, do they feel a distinct immunity to these charms that at any other time would make them proud? Why would they like this moppet a great deal better if her head were resting on a pillow instead of nodding up and down in agreement with Letterman? Because,

★ It's late,

★ Children should be in bed at this hour,

★ Parents deserve some peace and quiet,

★ This has gone on for two weeks straight, and

★ They don't know what to do.

When last seen, Mom and Dad were dozing off on couch and chair, respectively. Melissa was happily surfing stations with the remote control.

Those of us dealing with the postcrib set usually walk a middle ground between fairy tales and late, late shows. We have learned that preschoolers do not go to bed simply because it's time and we want them to. For the sake of survival on both sides, we've had to find ways to persuade our children to accept the daily inevitability of going to bed and getting to sleep. We have learned these measures partly from books, partly from friends and family, but mostly through trial and error. If these methods take into account our rights as parents and the individuality of our children, *and* they work, then we are probably on the right track.

The process of getting kids to bed can be a labyrinthine one, fraught with many possible wrong turns.

The Process

Kids have found artful ways to delay the process, wreak havoc with our timing, and thus forestall the inevitable. In the belief that bad bedtime habits can be broken and good ones substituted, let's turn to the specifics.

Stage One: The Preparation

Parents need to prepare for the preparation. It is helpful to have some basics already established.

★ How much sleep do the children actually need? We parents might prefer a twelve-hour snoozer, but we may have been blessed with a nine-hours-is-plenty bundle of energy. Bedtime hours may have to be adjusted to this fact. On the delicate question of naps, we know the parent may need them, but does the child? If a three-and-a-half-year-old suddenly starts protesting vociferously at the mere mention of slipping into pj's, perhaps a reduced naptime or a later bedtime is in order.

★ What are the ground rules? Children cooperate better when there are fairly consistent patterns of bedtime ritual. How long can they play outside after dinner? After what TV shows do they go to bed? Is there a bath almost every night? This is not to suggest that when Aunt Jenny comes for supper, the children must be whisked away from the table because bedtime is 7:30 P.M. Our busy lives require flexibility. But, in general, there is comfort in routine.

★ What foods, if any, seem to make our children hyperactive and sleepless? When identified, these foods can be greatly reduced in the diet or at least not offered for dinner.

★ How much physical exercise and fresh air do the children seem to need to put them in a relaxed frame of mind after dinner?

Revolutionary Rhetoric

At the child's actual time of going to bed, parents must deal with various forms of "Heck, no, we won't go!" These protests are often just part of the script; however, they are also a result of real disappointment about having to stop an enjoyable activity. We understand this. But we also have the responsibility to see that our children get the rest they require.

Children can learn from experience that we will not be detoured by tantrums, sit-down strikes, or accusations of being the meanest parents on the block. A particular bedtime hour is a fact of life in our household. Our confidence in the validity of this requirement and our consistency in enforcing it will also help.

Everyone should be clear about the time that preparing for bed occurs. Then, parents can use short, declarative statements like, "It's eight o'clock," and assume that all parties know what *that* means. Older preschoolers can be taught to recognize where the hands are on the clock when it is bedtime.

With some children, giving them fair warning ensures quicker cooperation. "You can go out and play now, but in fifteen minutes, it will be time to come in." When we drop the bombshell, it won't be quite as much of a shock to their systems.

Sometimes a race or game can transfer energy from arguments about sleep to the rigors of competition. One father defuses complaints by crouching in a racing position and challenging, "On your mark, get set, GO!" or "I'm gonna beat you upstairs." Statements like "First one to the bedroom is the winner" are hard to resist as well.

Younger children, especially, enjoy being carried to the bedroom in funny ways: like an airplane (zoom, zoom), on shoulders, upside down, or via the elephant walk (walking on their hands while the parent holds their feet).

Creative baby-sitters have been known to play a special version of hide and seek. When it's their turn to hide, they head straight for the bedroom. How about that? Here we are!

Successfully crossing the first hurdle leads, hopefully, to the next.

Quick Changes

The donning of pajamas can take an hour or a few minutes, depending on the luck of the evening and the success of our encouragements. Instead of the classic argument provoker—"Get your pajamas on, NOW!"—how about these possibilities?

★ Use reverse psychology. "I bet you can't get your pj's on before I finish the alphabet (or count to twenty)." The race is on.

★ Use more reverse psychology. "I'm leaving the room for a minute. Please, whatever you do, don't put your pajamas on. I'll get really upset if you put them on while I'm out of the room. And when I get upset, I tickle!" Sheer anticipation gets them moving.

★ Clown around by ripping socks and shoes off one at a time and hurl them around the room, making wild gestures but keeping in mind where the lamps are. This is quite effective with younger children.

Winding Down

The relaxing process can now begin. Stories, songs, and books work well here. The advantage is that drowsiness is fostered. Some parents allow a short amount of television time at this point. The advantage is that preparations are usually carried out with all deliberate speed so as not to miss the beginning of a favorite program. Other parents find workable a "get ready for bed, then we'll talk about your day" approach. The advantage is the establishment of a regular appointment for communication during which the child receives one hundred percent of the parent's attention. Combinations of the above can work too. The point is that spending some time creating a restful mood may often save time in the end.

Stage Two: The Big Event

We're all well acquainted with these stalling techniques: chasing brothers and sisters, jumping on beds, wanting just one more story, needing to go (once again) to the bathroom, then feeling the need to replace the lost liquid with just one more glass of water. A checklist can be helpful to diffuse the stalling. Before anybody hops in bed, the troops are polled.

★ Does everyone have the necessary blankets, bears, and pillows?

★ If anyone is parched from thirst, the water carriers are making their final rounds.

★ If anyone feels nature's call, there is no time like the present!

After attempting to settle the lighting issue to everyone's satisfaction—finding out whose night-light or closet light must be on and refereeing between those who *must* have the hall light on and those who can't sleep a wink with it on—parents are now in the enviable position of dispensing final farewells.

Except, somebody is likely to say, "I'm not tired," or

"I'm scared," or "My mosquito bites are itching, my bruises are aching, my ears are ringing, my nose is dripping. How can I possibly go to sleep in such agony?" At this point, parents sigh and resurrect other options.

The Drill Sergeant Approach

"Everyone will, on the count of three, be asleep." However, unless the child is unusually malleable, this doesn't work. It is a challenge to challenge our authority and a command we cannot enforce. We can insist that a child stay in her room, but sleep comes only to those who let it.

The "Good Things Come to Those Who Sleep" Approach

"All those who cooperate and let themselves fall asleep will find a goodie near their beds in the morning, compliments of the goodie fairy." Perhaps this is bribery. We prefer to think of it as behavior modification. This can be used until good bedtime habits are established, at which point the rhythms of routine should take over.

The "Be Responsible for Relaxing Yourself to Sleep" Approach

With a few minor restrictions, the child may look at books, color, or draw designs until sleepy. The few minor restrictions include: absolutely no loud singing, chanting, or laughing while working; no conversation with fellow sleep resisters; no loud turning of pages; no using squeaky crayons; no rustling of paper. They get tired just reviewing the rules! A bonus is that they do learn to be responsible for themselves in this area.

The "We're in This Thing Together" Approach

A parent may opt to sit in the room until the child falls asleep. If you choose this alternative, be prepared for any or all of the following events: being asked if *you* are asleep every thirty seconds; being sung to; developing lower backache and fanny fatigue; or tiptoeing from the room and hearing, "Fooled you! I'm still awake." This approach can be comforting when a child is especially bothered by nighttime fears, but it is not recommended for nightly use.

Stage Three: The Follow-Up and Still Other Scenarios

Once the kids are tucked in, there is possibly one stage left to go. Two basic scenarios are involved here.

Wee Willie Winkie Ran Upstairs and Down

Any self-respecting preschooler can think up a million reasons for an absolutely mandatory exit from the bedroom and entrance into whatever room her parents happen to be occupying.

★ To inform us what horrible things a sibling is doing, but she's not

★ To show us a work of art so splendid it could not possibly wait for a morning showing

★ To remind us of a game we promised to play with her a week ago Tuesday and didn't

★ To notify us that her pillowcase has a big, huge hole in it (which we find to be of a size that an electron microscope might be able to detect)

★ To pose a question that vitally affects her current and future welfare: "Can I wear my red socks tomorrow?"

When I'm Calling You-oo-oo-oo, Will You Answer Too?

Instead of appearing in person, the child telegraphs her pressing concerns from the bedroom door, hoping that her parents will respond, "We can't hear you. Come here and tell us."

Depending on our individual tolerance for post-bedtime interaction with our children, some of us may accept one visitation but deem two as the limit of our end-of-the-day indulgence. Here are some options for encouraging the bedded to stay bedded. We can:

★ State our displeasure with wanderings. "It is time to sleep. I don't appreciate your getting out of bed. I don't want to see you out here again." Determine ahead of time what to do if you *do* see her again.

★ Ignore the calls or the child's physical presence. However, if this method does not have an immediate discouraging impact, we might be in for trouble. The child may think we just don't hear her and yell loud enough to wake the rest of the house, if not the neighborhood. Or, the child may think we just don't notice and plop herself on our lap, meeting us nose to nose.

★ Indicate our displeasure by carrying the interloper immediately back to bed, while refusing to engage in any conversation. Literally, do not say a word. It's no fun to interlope on a mummy.

★ Outline the consequences of persistence in this behavior. "This is our grown-up time. You are interrupting it. You are taking away one of our privileges. I guess we'll have to take away one of yours, such as visiting Johnny Reed tomorrow." Remember that when you use threats like this, you must be willing and able to back them up.

★ Employ a stopgap measure, take the coward's way out, or pass the buck. In the hope that this is just a stage the child is going through, we can arrange recurrent, pressing nighttime meetings and leave the bedtime hassle to our spouse or an unsuspecting sitter.

Speaking of passing the buck, whatever happened to the sandman? Didn't he always do this work for parents?

Index

Acceptable vs. unacceptable
   behavior, 26, 34–35
Adult temper tantrums,
   77–82
Apologies, 81
Apron strings, 54–57
Arbitration, 63–65
Authoritarian approach, 87

Baby-sitters
   maternity hospital stay
      and, 18
   television and, 128
Bait and switch, 12
Bargaining, 86
Bedtime, 153–63
   calling and, 161–63
   donning of pajamas, 158

exit from bedroom and,
   161
preparation for, 156–57
protests and, 157–58
stalling techniques and,
   159–60
winding down for, 158–59
Bullies, 66–68

Car travel, 144–46
Clean plate club, 86–87
Compromise
   fighting and, 65–66
   telephone calls and,
      117–19
Concession, 13–14
Conscience, 97–98
Crayons, 50

Discipline, 33–44
  acceptable vs. unaccept-
    able concept in, 34–35
  blow-ups and, 41–43
  child-created situations
    and, 37–39
  control in, 43–44
  distance in, 39
  easing up in, 38
  expanded withdrawal
    tactic and, 38
  fairness in, 40
  grouchy parents and,
    40–41
  housework and, 39–40
  "no" in, 35–37
  parent-created situations
    and, 39–41
  stubborness and, 41
  withdrawal tactic in,
    37–38
Diversionary tactic, 12
Doctors' and dentists'
  offices, 142–44

Eating habits, 83–89
  authoritarian approach
    and, 87
  bargaining and, 86
  bedtime and, 156
  clean plate club and,
    86–87
  ground rules and, 89
  snacks and, 91–95
  teaching nutritional
    concepts and,
    93–95
Expanded withdrawal tactic,
  38

Fairness, 40
Fighting, 59–68
  arbitration in, 63–65
  bullies and underdogs in,
    66–68
  compromise and, 65–66
  determining cause of, 61
  stories and, 62–63
  verbal vs. physical expres-
    sion in, 62
Forced exit, 10–11

Giving in, 78–79
Good job technique, 119
Goofy, the, 11–12
Grocery store, 140–41
Guilt trips, 81

Hitters, 25–27
Home birth, 17–18
Housework, 39–40
Hugs, 82

"I" approach, 10
"I feel" technique, 9–10
Ignore tactic, 9
Imagination, 98–99, 103
Inanimate objects, hitting,
  26–27, 62, 80

"Just a minute" technique,
  118

Lying, 97–105

"Me want bottle, too" child,
  29
Misdirected playmate pusher,
  29–30

Naggers, 45, 47–48
Name-callers, 69–71
Naps, 156
Necessary outings, 136,
    140–44
"No," 35–37

One-way streeters, 30–31
Opportunist misbehavers,
    28–29
Optional outings, 136–37,
    149–52
Outings, 133–52
  advance preparation for,
    137–38
  car travel and, 144–46
  to doctors' and dentists'
    offices, 142–44
  fair expectations in,
    137
  to friends and relatives,
    148–49
  to grocery store, 140–41
  ignoring expectations of
    others, 139
  necessary, 136, 140–44
  needs of youngest child in,
    138–39
  optional, 136–37, 149–52
  paying attention to chil-
    dren during, 139
  plane travel and, 146–48
  positive reinforcement
    and, 139–40
  probably necessary, 136,
    145–48
  protecting host's home,
    148–49
  to restaurants, 149–51

shopping trips, 141–43
to special places, 151–52

Parent hitters, 30
Parental example
  name-calling and, 69–70
  television watching and,
    127–28
  whining and, 46
Plane travel, 146–48
Preschoolers, 49–57
  apron strings and, 54–57
  crayons and, 50
  ransacking and, 51–52
  street safety for, 52–54
  telephone calls and, 118
  television and, 125–26
Probably necessary outings,
    136, 145–48

Ransacking, 51–52
Restaurants, 149–51
Retreat, 12–13

"Say hi to grandma" tech-
    nique, 118–19
Seethers, 28–29
Sharing, 73–75
Shopping trips, 141–42
Sibling preparation classes,
    17
Sibling rivalry, 15–23
  first impression of new
    baby and, 19–21
  hitters and, 25–27
  "Me want bottle, too"
    child and, 29
  misdirected playmate
    pusher and, 29–30

one-way streeters and,
30–31
opportunist misbehavers
and, 28–29
parent hitters and, 30
preparation for new baby
and, 17–19
seethers and, 28–29
sulkers and, 28–29
toilet-trained sudden
wetters and, 27–28
Snacks, 91–95
Special places, outings to,
151–52
Stealing, 107–11
Stories, 62–63
Street safety, 52–54
Stress, 78
Stubborness, 41
Sulkers, 28–29

Tattlers, 71–72
Telephone calls, 113–21
competition with, 114–15
compromise and,
117–19
explaining purpose of,
116–17
good job technique and,
119
incoming, 115–16

"just a minute" technique
and, 118
placing child before,
119–20
"say hi to grandma" tech-
nique and, 118–19
Television, 123–31
babies and, 124–25
bedtime and, 159
flexibility and, 130
house rules for watching,
126–28
older children and, 129–30
preschoolers and, 125–26
Television commercials,
125–26
Toilet-trained sudden
wetters, 27–28

Unacceptable behavior. *See*
Acceptable vs. unaccept-
able behavior
Underdogs, 66–68

Verbal expression of anger,
62, 79–80
Visits to friends and
relatives, 148–49

Whiners, 45, 46
Withdrawal tactic, 37–38